DELUGE

THE GREAT FLOOD OF THE BIBLE

DANIEL ELTZROTH

CONTENTS

Introduction

THE BIBLE'S FIRST BOOK, the book of Genesis, contains within it the narrative of the Deluge, the Great Flood of Noah and the Ark. While one of the best known of Old Testament episodes, it has over the centuries been presented unevenly, sounding at times stilted and too 'biblical.' Compounding that, other than brief explanations of a few sections or a few verses, a deep reaching, detailed examination of the complete narrative has been needed.

To help resolve this, genuinely investigating the 'What did it once really say?' aspect of the entirety of its ancient wording now can resolve the many unclear passages and bring back to the forefront its once easily obvious elements.

The focus here is to return to the original telling, which in antiquity was presented aloud. It was audience-based, and meant to be heard rather than read. By returning to that perspective, its well-formulated composition can again become more fully recognizable. This work takes a close look at the verbal pattern of design of the chronicle, and is accompanied by a new translation, one attuned to its cultural origins yet made clear-cut through accessible phrasing.

The translated portion of this work (chapters two and three, which are then shown lyrically in chapter fifteen) brings the narrative up to date in contemporary voice. At the same time it adheres to the original approach in pacing, its text observing as closely as possible the coordinated, cadenced style, one familiar to those of long ago.

The work in those chapters two and three is in modern conventional paragraph style. But, when quoted in all later chapters, the referenced verses are printed, line-by-line, in lyric form. While they are the same words, one may observe that the lines 'look' non-traditional as compared to a primary sentence and paragraph-set. This is by design, to closely replicate the once clipped, short phrasing, and staccato-like composition.

Much of the intensity of this ancient narrative came from its brevity. An updated presentation can frequently attempt to embellish, and thus to consequently begin a subtle departure from the original. Here in this book the elaboration upon what had become, over time, sometimes vague, occurs not within that wording itself, but in the descriptive chapters which follow. It is there that the explanations take place. There the verbiage is traced through the ages, first through the original terms, then through later classic works, and finally through the centuries of changing English. Those earlier adaptations serve as instructive guideposts to determining accuracy.

Now, to bring about what the Great Flood epic was saying, the back-to-the-basics meanings of those texts are revitalized, yielding a work which, as it spoke to bygone times, can speak tellingly to these times.

Daniel Eltzroth

1

A Mirrored Pattern

FOR A SPEAKER or author of long ago, one of the better means to convey powerful ideas within a long descriptive account was through the use of *chiasma*, or verbal *crossings*. The term refers to a phrase or to a sustained sequence, one which is first presented directly and then is echoed by being repeated in reverse order, with each idea reflected back in mirror form. A method popular in early storytelling, it remains in use to this day.

As a brief example, the phrase: 'When the going gets tough, the tough get going' is chiastic, since the sentence states and then reverses the three key words: going, get(s), and tough, and the duplicating style allows the catchphrase to be more readily remembered. With each focus word lettered for clarity, the format is: abc-cba. The singular term *chiasm* derives from the Greek letter Chi, written like the letter 'X', the symbol itself suggesting the verbal intersection.

In longer and more complex variations, many multiple phrases and even pages, chapters, and entire plots have been framed around this pattern, regularly defined by a center point, conventionally labelled with the X, functioning as the turnaround: abcXcba. That central phrasing would traditionally contain a key element, a nucleus of emphasis about which the other ordered segments lead to and from.

Such an approach was a reliable and effective assist to long-form memorization, aiding orators of antiquity in recalling the significant moments of a complex chronicle while reciting before multiple audiences, with repeating sections even being sung. Smaller internal supporting chiasms could also be positioned within larger ones, with thousands of lines of content being powerfully depicted by those skilled in presentation.

By adhering to a circular course, the impact upon listeners was increased through the reinforcing of prior details, and any telling, irrespective of length, constructed in this design would be enhanced by the progression and then retrogression of continuity. The style is found throughout the Bible, highlighting advice, admonitions, and episodic passages.

Moving specifically to the Great Flood narrative, it was written as one wide-ranging chiasm, and within it were nested smaller internal repeats.

Also, rather than strictly a portrayal of the actions of Noah, who is silent throughout, the episode is largely a portrayal of the thoughts and accompanying actions of God, including entrusting Noah with the many tasks of responsibility.

It is the expressed thought processes, followed by the world-defining acts of God which are the instrumentality of the narrative, and which propel the entire dynamic. The passages unfold sequentially, with a well-established beginning *(the selection of Noah and initiating the flood)*, then later a crucial midpoint *(the ceasing of the rising waters)*, and finally a heartening conclusion *(the assurances of no future worldwide flood)*. At each juncture, there is first a purposeful observation/contemplation which is then followed by a momentous action.

For simplicity, the outline below is a brief synopsis of the full chronicle, in the structure of the original. Providing a representation of its pacing and style, it can be encapsulated as:

a) God observed, then decided:
Those of wrongful living,
Throughout the world,
Should no longer survive.

b)   God selected Noah:
   To construct an Ark,
   To be stocked with animals,
   Each to be kept alive.

c)   A massive flood proceeded.

x)   Later, God ceased
      The rising of the seas.

c)   Slowly the water receded.

b)   God instructed Noah:
   All were to depart,
   To increase in numbers,
   That each may thrive.

a) God stated this Promise:
Such a flood
To encompass the world
Shall never again arrive.

In the next two chapters the Biblical Flood epic is presented in its entirety, translated from scripture. For clarity, a few archaic terms have been updated, such as *cubits* to feet. Yet in full, this narrative tightly adheres to the early conceptions, such as torrents of water being released upon the earth's surface, from below and above, rather than rainfall. Those and similar phrasings are explained in greater detail in the subsequent chapters.

This work endeavors, while retaining a scrupulous adherence to literal meaning, to closely reflect what a listener, in their place and time, would have heard then, in rhythmical language from an orator reciting before a group. Here, the next chapter contains the first two Genesis sections, the advancement of the Deluge, and the chapter following contains the Flood's cessation and withdrawal. It begins at Genesis 6, with verse 5.

2

The Fate of the World,
The Deluge Begins

Genesis VI and VII

^{6:5} **The Lord God** began to look closely at what was becoming an intensifying hostility, one inhabiting every individual, all over the world. Their course of thought, unfolding from within each heart, was of nothing but wrongdoing, day after day. ⁶ So it was, that God reflected on having created people upon the earth.

After profound deliberation, ⁷ God spoke: "I am about to sweep aside humanity, those I have formed, any to be seen on earth. Gone will be the humans, and further, the animals, from crawling beasts up to the birds of the sky. This, the result of my decision to have brought them into being."

⁸ However, one had attained the approval of the Lord God. ⁹ There was Noah.

Noah: Righteous, a man of integrity among the others of his time, highly regarded by God.

[10] Noah, a father of three sons, named: Shem, Ham, and Japheth.

[11] But still, in the very sight of God, desecration was engulfing the world; deceit, overtaking the world. [12] The Lord God was witnessing the earth's regions approaching ruin. The one correct course was being utterly abandoned by those living all across the lands.

[13] And it was then the Lord God disclosed to Noah: "A breaking point for human beings has been reached here before me. It is certain that, spreading from them, the earth is being severely defiled. Now listen well: I bring an end to this, to the world as it is.

[14] "For this reason you, yourself, will be building an Ark. Begin with squared timbers of wood. Bind together beams to be aligned within the Ark, and seal with securing veneer what will be the inside and out. [15] You shall then lay out the Ark to this: Five hundred feet the length of the Ark, eighty feet its width, fifty feet to be its height. [16] To join together the Ark: You will raise it, and closely connect it at its crowning point. Also, a door you shall install in the side of the Ark, and with a ground floor, a second floor, and a third, you shall make it ready.

[17] "Know this: I will be inflicting a flood of water onto the earth, to lay waste to all beings which take in their breath of life from beneath the sky. As many as there are upon the earth, each shall meet an early end.

[18] "Yet, as to you, I put forward this lasting Agreement: You will be permitted to stay within that Ark, you and your sons, and your wife, and the wives of your sons with you.

[19] "Furthermore – From among all the beasts of burden, all the crawling serpents, all untamed of the wild, from all those that exist, two by two from every one of these, you are to guide them into that Ark, where you are to provide

for them, male and female, alive, there with you. ²⁰ Of the birds according to their lineage, livestock separated by their sort, creatures which crawl upon the ground according to their groups, two by two from all of these will be approaching there, for you to take in, each male and female. ²¹ And you are to gather all types of food to eat. Collect it together, to sustain yourself and each of them."

²² And Noah carried through on every part of this. What the Lord God had commanded of him, he did accomplish.

Genesis VII

7:1   **And then the Lord God** said to Noah: "You are to enter! You and your entire family into the Ark, for under my observance: You are of preeminent character in the midst of these times.

² "Now – To the clean livestock, those which are pure for ritual, those you shall guide in, seven by seven, male and female. But of the unclean, those two by two, male and female each. ³ And even the birds of the sky: Of the clean, seven by seven, male and female paired. Of the birds unclean, two by two, male, female, to assure the spread of seed across all the lands.

⁴ "It is to be, in seven days, I will deliver a devastation of water to the world, forty days and forty nights. I will wash away every entity I have made from the entire surface of the earth."

⁵ And again, all that the Lord God commanded of him, Noah accomplished. ⁶ This, while Noah himself was six hundred years of age, and the earth about to be subjected to a crushing deluge.

⁷ Nonetheless, Noah, with his sons, and his wife, and his sons' wives, made their way to within the Ark, to hold out against the waters of the forthcoming flood. ⁸ Also, from among the clean birds of flight and the unclean birds, of the clean livestock and livestock unclean, of the clean

wildlife and the unclean, [9] they went into the Ark, in toward Noah, male and female, each two by two, in accordance with the directives of God. [10] And so, after seven days, the tumultuous flood was set in force upon the world.

[11] It being the six hundredth year of Noah's life, in its second month, on the twenty seventh day of the month, on that day:

Burst apart all the bulging reservoirs buried deep below, and towering enclosures holding oceans above the skies flung open. [12] Waters were released onto the earth, forty days and forty nights.

[13] During that first day, having entered into the Ark, were: Noah, his sons Shem, Ham, Japheth, and Noah's wife, and the three wives of his sons. [14] And then, every untamed beast by their species, all livestock by their sort, crawling creatures by their categories, winged birds from their flocks, [15] they came, conducted by Noah, into the Ark, two by two, male and female, from all branches of beings which embody the breath of life. [16] Those entering, each male and female, each entity of existence embarked in the same manner as God had directed to Noah. And with that, the Lord God shut the Ark from the outside.

[17] The flooding kept on those forty days and forty nights. The waters advanced, uplifting the Ark, elevating it high above the surroundings. [18] The unrestricted overflow ranged ever further, immersing the lands, carrying the Ark upon its waves. [19] The waters, seemingly without end, came to conceal the expanses, overspreading every one of the mountains under the heavens. [20] The levels grew to twenty five feet above the highest peaks. [21] And so perished all the living which had before been active across the vast regions: Birds, livestock, animals of the wild, crawling serpents, all which moved over the surface; and with them, every person. [22] They that had breathed with spirit of life, they, anywhere upon the lands, all passed away. [23] Taken from existence was their every trace off the

face of the earth: From humans, animals, crawling serpents, and birds of the sky. None any longer were alive in the world. Only remaining were Noah and those with him inside the Ark.

[24] And the waters stood at those heights upon the earth one hundred and fifty days.

3

The Flooding is Stopped,
A Return to Land

VIII and IX
Of Genesis

8:1 **And it was, t**hat God came to bring back to mind Noah, all the untamed beasts, all the livestock, all the winged birds, all the crawling serpents, the many, there with him inside the Ark. And it was then that God proceeded to bring forth a transcendent breath of wind across the world, which calmed the water. ² And so, were set firm: Both the reservoirs from the deep below, and the enclosures above the sky. Further inundation from the heavens was held back. ³ It followed, that after one hundred and fifty days, the waters coursing over the earth then were drawing away, their levels dropped lower.

⁴ In the seventh month, on the twenty seventh day, the Ark came to a halt above the mountains of Ararat. ⁵ With

lapping waters in gradual decline, and when the passing days reached the first of the tenth month, the peaks of the mountains had reappeared.

⁶ There, after forty days had passed, Noah opened the small window within the Ark he himself had built. ⁷ He released one raven, one, to see how much the waters were reduced. But it only darted away, not to return until later, after the world had fully dried. ⁸ So he sent out a dove to succeed it, to discover if water was withdrawn from the land. ⁹ When the dove could not catch sight of any resting place to perch, it flew back to him at the Ark, for water still stood over the wide expanses of the earth. Noah, reaching out his hand, took hold of the dove and brought it inside the Ark. ¹⁰ After waiting seven days, he again released the dove. ¹¹ When it came back with a fresh olive leaf in its beak, Noah realized the waters were no longer extending over all regions. ¹² He waited another seven days, once more sent out the dove, and that time it did not return.

¹³ And it came to be, Noah reached in his life the age of six hundred and one. In that same month, on the first day of the month, the water had receded from more of the world. Noah uncovered the roof of the Ark he had built and could see for himself: Water was lowering over the face of the earth. ¹⁴ In the next, the second month, on the twenty seventh day of the month, the land's surface had become fully dry.

¹⁵ Then the Lord God spoke to Noah, saying: ¹⁶ "Proceed forth, out from the Ark: You, your wife, your sons, your sons' wives with you! ¹⁷ And all the living: The birds, the livestock, the wild animals of the ground, lead them out as well. Then, grow greater in numbers, spread throughout the earth!" ¹⁸ And emerged: Noah and his wife, and his sons, and the wives of his sons with him. ¹⁹ And every wild beast, the livestock, the winged birds, the crawling creatures, according to their type, all departed the Ark.

²⁰ Then Noah built an altar to the Lord. He selected from among all the clean livestock, and from among all the clean birds, and set those as burnt offerings upon that sacred place. ²¹ The Lord sensed the sweet fragrance, and thus the Lord God decided: "In giving thought, I will not compound the condemnation of the lands of the earth, despite the dealings of humanity. And while the notions of human beings still incline toward the wrongdoing of youth, I will not again strike down all the living in such manner as I have done.

²² "As long as the earth exists, planting and harvest, cold and heat, spring and summer, day and night, shall not be taken away."

Genesis IX

9:1 **And God** delivered blessings upon Noah and his sons, and said to them: "Grow in numbers, fill the world, exercise authority over it. ² From here forward: Aversion, a trembling fright of you, will exist within every beast of the land, every bird of the sky, in all which slide along the ground, to within the fish of every sea. Into your hands I offer them. ³ Each living creature can now be food for you, as have been the fields of vegetables I had placed before all of you.

⁴ "But if their lifeblood still moves within, do not eat of them. ⁵ So shall it be with your blood, yours, of your very soul. Were it to be slashed from within you by the claw of any savage animal, I shall hold that beast to account. And just as much so, were it, from any person, to be spilled by the hand even of one's brother, I shall hold that man to account. ⁶ For anyone ever to shed the blood of a human being, so shall that one's blood be shed in return. It is thus, in the unassailable Image of God, I made mankind.

⁷ "But now, you yourselves: Grow in numbers, multiply, spread out and fill the earth."

[8] Continuing, God spoke to Noah and to his sons with him, saying, [9] "Know this: I stand forth to uphold my promise made to you, and to your descendants after you, [10] and also to every living being after you, from the birds, from the livestock, from all the wild beasts of the world, as many as accompanied you, all those sent out from inside the Ark. [11] I shall stand by this promise to you: Never again shall all flesh cease from the water of the flood. Never again shall there be a flood of water to devastate the world."

[12] Then God spoke further to Noah: "This becomes the symbol of that pledge I enter upon with you, and with every living creature, as many as will be for unending generations. [13] I unfurl this rainbow among the clouds, it will be a display of the sacred pledge between myself and the earth. [14] And it shall be, wherever I gather clouds over the earth and a rainbow shall be seen, [15] then I will remember my promise between myself and you, and between every living being: Never again shall the water of a flood take away all that live.

[16] "When a rainbow is in the clouds, I will look upon it and shall remember the everlasting promise between myself and the earth, and between living beings of all flesh throughout the world." [17] And God said to Noah: "That shall be the visible confirmation of this decree which I have proclaimed between myself and all the living upon the earth."

[18] The sons of Noah who departed the Ark were Shem, and Ham, and Japheth. Ham was the father of Canaan. [19] And these three, the sons of Noah, were from whom their descendants disbursed throughout the lands.

4

Ancient Sources, Ancient Terms

FOR THE WORDING of the Flood chronicle in its particulars, the earliest available sources will be referenced. Of those existing in antiquity, Hebrew and Aramaic scrolls, none have survived in original form. However, from many centuries later, Hebrew copies from those sources have been sustained through Masoretic texts (the word *Masorete* is derived from an Aramaic word meaning Tradition Keeper) of the 6th to 10th centuries of the current, modern era (CE/AD), methodically transcribed from more ancient texts.

Also, surviving from much earlier, what does remain of the initial books of biblical scripture, having been compiled around the third century BCE, the oldest existing translation of the first five books of the Bible (called the Books of Moses), is the Greek *Septuagint*. It has come to be known by that name, adopted later, by using the Latin term for 'seventy' or the Roman numeral LXX, for the number of experts traditionally believed to have been involved in the project.

It was a compilation from earlier scrolls into Alexandrian dialect, or the Hellenistic (also called Koine, meaning *common*) Greek of Egypt. In that immediate post-Alexander the Great era, Greek had become extensively exercised, often as a second language, in both writing and commerce throughout the Mediterranean region. After that project had been completed, the additional scriptural books, those beyond the first five, were translated into Greek by others throughout the next two centuries. Within Christianity, in Eastern Orthodoxy, the full Septuagint has consistently remained the basis of the Old Testament, and through modern translation, continues there to remain so.

Inevitably, and relating to the flood episode specifically, some variations in wording between the Hebrew and Greek versions do exist, and are examined as this book proceeds.

Another long-surviving work, also consulted here, in the language of Latin, is the Vulgate translation of the Bible. A late fourth century translation derived from even earlier Latin texts, as well as from the Greek Septuagint and Hebrew texts, it came to be referred to as the *versio vulgate* or the *version commonly-used.* Intended for the average individual, not merely scholars, it was readable in widely-spoken language. It became the standard in Western Christianity and continued to be in use worldwide for over a thousand years. Its styling and root words clearly impacted the English translations which came about much later.

Those earliest English works will also be referenced and quoted from, as their ground-breaking verbiage carries forward to most modern editions. The oldest English translation cited here is that of the fourteenth century theologian John Wycliffe, a British scholar and professor at (early) Oxford University. He introduced a series of Bible translations into the popular vernacular, Middle

English, which were completed by 1395, and were based upon the Latin Vulgate Bible.

Over a century later, another English scholar, William Tyndale, made it his life's work to also translate the Bible into English, to allow it to be more widely shared. Inspired by the German biblical translation of Martin Luther, Tyndale based his work not only on the Latin Vulgate, but also upon the Hebrew and Greek versions which by those times were becoming more available. In that tumultuous religious era, Tyndale was forced into exile for his translations which he published from Germany, and was hunted down by authorities and ultimately executed for heresy in 1536, indicating the highly volatile nature of such work. His reputation was posthumously reinstated somewhat, due to a renewed and belated recognition of the significance of his achievements a few years later as they had by then become more widely read and respected. His revised edition of the book of Genesis had been completed in 1534.

In the same century, the Geneva Bible, another translation of the entire Bible, was produced, and was so named for the Swiss city to which its translators had fled by reason of continuing religious persecution in mid-sixteenth century England. The first full edition was published in 1560, and was ground breaking in that it was the first in English to employ numbered verses. Becoming the authoritative Bible for influential writers of the time (including Shakespeare), there were 150 subsequent editions over the next century. Popular for its vigorous language, but in some quarters controversial for its expanded marginal notes, which were viewed an anti-monarchical, it was superseded over time by a separate version more satisfactory to the government, the King James Version (KJV) of 1611, which in proceeding centuries became the standard in English.

Each of these versions will be briefly quoted from, to examine various aspects of interpretation concerning the

Flood episode, and to show how differentiations in the expressiveness have unfolded over the centuries.

To begin with primary word usage, in the Greek flood account there were three separate wordings for God, expressed by either the use of *the Lord God, God,* or *the Lord.* For those designations in Hebrew scripture, its text utilized for the first, the Lord God, the formal *Yahweh* (the proper name for God) and for the second, *Elohim* (Creator, the power over powers).

In Greek, to make those differentiations, there is the term *kurios,* meaning Lord, or master, or sir. Also there is *Theos,* meaning *God the Creator* and Supreme Being, and is retained as a root in English in such words as *theology* and *theocracy.* For *Yahweh,* in Greek the term *theos* was combined with *kurios,* and the two terms were written connectedly as 'the Lord God.' At the start of the narrative, the first two verses used the joined terms, as in 6:5, *"The Lord God* began" and then the single term in 6:6, *"God* reflected." Much further in the narrative, at 8:21 was the solitary word for the *Lord,* with: "The *Lord* sensed the sweet fragrance."

Within the entire ancient episode, as presented in the preceding two chapters, many of its expressions were repeated in its stylized back and forth method. That compositional approach allows the smaller connecting components to strengthen the view of the grander picture. It can be compared in artistic outline to a large mural, one displaying a series of scenes within the larger thematic portrait. Intertwined within were first many internally repeated, and then later reversed recitations, which added depth and detail by relaying images through a variety of echoed phrasings, giving evidence of having been intricately arranged.

There has long been commentary asserting that there are inconsistencies throughout the narrative. For example, it has been asked how is it that the same statements and events are listed many times, over and over, and with some variations. One long standing supposition has been that the episode is a fusion or a hybridization of two related but not identical earlier versions, subsequently merged together.

A perhaps more simple answer, notwithstanding being theorized as a series of additions or insertions by different or later authors, is that when viewed lyrically, those repetitions can be acknowledged as a part of a unified rhetorical construct. Much of the verbal framework can be viewed as paired (a statement then a restatement) or as three-fold (a subject, then a counterbalancing subject, then back to the original subject), or as both, within certain longer sequences, using slightly different phrasing. These types of recurrences, when delivered as part of an oral tradition, constitute refrains, intended at intervals to return to, and to continually stress significant developments. Duplications, with separate details, in any telling can exist as stylistic features, and as a formulated whole, the written flood account conforms to this type of intentionally configured template.

To take a more intensive look at the initiating verses of the narrative, from here on all the verses will be positioned in lyrical formatting, to visually replicate the word emphasis of oration. Long ago recorded into scroll form, in the absence of accents or punctuation, many of the strategic pauses of an ancient presenter can be easily missed, especially when placed in a long sentence structure.

Instead, listed here will be the same words, now introduced and arranged throughout this book in a more clipped, shorter line by line form. When being read in that format, the tempo, the natural stops, the cadences in phrasing, the script-like structure, each comes through more effectively. With that, it can more strictly recreate those once spoken words, and an orator's pacing can in a

sense again be realized. Here, for example, the first three
verses are:

6:5)   The Lord God
Began to look closely
At what was becoming
An intensifying hostility,
One inhabiting every individual,
All over the world.
Their course of thought,
Unfolding from within each heart,
Was of nothing but wrongdoing,
Day after day.
6) So it was,
That God reflected:
On having created
People upon the earth.
After profound deliberation,
7) God spoke:
"I am about
To sweep aside
Humanity,
Those I have formed,
Any to be seen on earth.
Gone
Will be the humans,
And further,
The animals,
From crawling beasts,
Up to the birds of the sky.
This,
The result of my decision
To have brought them
Into being."

Many of the ancient articulated word formations
occurring in the course of the entire episode are made

evident in these very first verses. For example, the third verse, 6:7, in a distinct manner sums up much of the entire remaining narrative. Within it are listed many of the keywords (God, the earth, the sky, humanity, animals) which repeat as the events unfold.

Successive word associations take place in this verse, as do many others throughout. Here, the pairing of *from* and *to* are in consecutive lines:

> *From* crawling beasts,
> Up *to* the birds of the sky

These add to a back and forth styling, as do the oppositional matchings of *humans* and *animals*, and the ground-based *crawling beasts* contrast with *birds of the sky*.

Before that, the first verse, 6:5, begins in the narrator's words, that God "began to look closely at" the heightening hostility amidst individuals.

For explanatory purposes, and delving into the ancient wording, the actual term used for *look closely* (Hebrew *raah*, Greek *eidō*) connoted a perception by sense, that is, of seeing with the eyes, of scrutinizing through observation. Beyond that, it meant *to see about*, as from one who wishes to focus attention upon a circumstance, a fact-finding in order to ascertain what has been taking place. A term used in more recent centuries was 'to behold,' a word carrying a more significant impact than merely *to see*, and here, "to look closely" can introduce that more stringent type of survey. The verse was stressing the viewing of agitation, that which was originating from and increasing within human beings. It contains two phrases about perceived humanity, first a statement, "intensifying hostility," followed by a restatement, "nothing but wrongdoing."

Verse 6:6 then proceeds beyond that, inaugurating God's giving serious thought to the witnessed problem, with the wording both of "reflected on" and "profound deliberation." The third of the three verses continues by setting forth in God's words, now quoted in the first person, what God will be going to do, to what will be the direct actions resulting from the thought processes. This verse 6:7 contains what will be a forthcoming action, that God will "sweep aside" humans and animals. The three verses here are first of observation, closely perceiving what was taking place within people, of what their thoughts were manifesting, then resulting in a conclusion being made by God on how to resolve this.

Various terms over the centuries have been applied for that verb construct: "about to sweep aside." In the King James Version, it was: "I will destroy man whom I have created," wording which has been followed by many more recent versions, each frequently with the word *destroy*. The Geneva and Tyndale Bibles also had used *destroy*.

However, the Hebrew verb was *machah*, with more of an exacting meaning of: To erase, to *wipe out*, to cancel. In Greek, the verb comparably was *apalgeó*, again to wipe away, to *blot out*, pertaining in a practical manner to the removal of temporarily recorded characters, as on a wax tablet, those which could be erased, be brushed aside. The understood implication was, in those times, that there was first a tangible or intangible 'something' there, and then that 'something' could be expunged, taken away, and then potentially replaced, as a multi-part procedure.

The ancient verb, in both Hebrew and Greek, rather than harboring a solo meaning of destructiveness, alternatively carried more of an impression of the ephemeral, to dissipate. For example, the same verb in each language was used in Isaiah 44:22 as *put away*: "I have put away thy transgressions like a cloud, and thy sins as a mist" (Geneva Bible).

Clouds are not thought of as being destroyed. A single word, such as *destroy*, no longer as adequately reflects the ancient interpretation.

Moreover, the wording was being used at the very

beginning of the narrative, as a lead-up to an advancing step-wise series of instructions and events, part of the intensifying episodic nature of the chronicle.

Here, to invoke the early verbalism of a decision to dispel out of the way nearly all humanity, as with a wave of the hand, its original implications have been addressed with: "am about to sweep aside."

The three-verse opening segment begins with an awareness, then advances to serious thought, and is followed by a statement of decision, one describing the resolving action to be taken.

The commencing clause of each of the first three verses contains a preparatory statement (The Lord God began to look closely, God reflected, God spoke) to provide emphasis to each of the succeeding elaborating descriptions. As with a prominent oratorical pause after each brief preface, it can replicate a recitation protocol of earlier times.

A matching instance of this Awareness-Thought-Action procedure comes later, after all had departed the Ark, in one long verse at 8:21, where God became aware of Noah's offerings ("sensed the sweet fragrance") and gave thought ("in giving thought") and then decided, through fulfilling the pledge to never again send such a flood ("I will not again strike down.") Here is that entire verse:

> 8:21) The Lord
> Sensed the sweet fragrance,
> And thus
> The Lord God decided:
> "In giving thought,
> I will not
> Compound the condemnation
> Of the lands of the earth,
> Despite the dealings
> Of humanity.

And while the notions
Of human beings
Still incline toward
The wrongdoing of youth,
I will not again
Strike down
All the living
In such manner,
As I have done.

Also, situated between these widely separated verses, at the midpoint of the entire episode, another appearance of the purposeful process is at verse 8:1. There, in the midst of the flooding, it states that God recalled to mind Noah ("came to bring back to mind") and then acted to calm the waters ("proceeded to bring forth a transcendent breath of wind.")

Each of these three processes sets up a critical juncture (prior to, during, and after the conclusion of the flood) and each introduced and established reinforcing details within the following segments, to expound upon the repercussions of each authoritative action. At each instance, a solution was determined and was followed up with a demonstrable active response.

It is this format, that of God becoming aware, giving careful thought, then moving toward a reciprocal series of actions, interlaced with commands to Noah, which largely defines the layout of the narrative.

In the early verses, here were described the thoughts and then actions of God, but also within them are the thought processes and actions of those being observed, the human beings of that time. Returning to the first two verses of the narrative, 6:5-6, the text alludes to the observed behavior, to the nature of humanity, to the increasing hostility.

Relating to thought, in Greek, two forms of the word

dianeuó (pronounced *dee-an-yoo´-o*), were used. In 6:5 it is stated, first for the flawed humans, as "their *course of thought unfolding*" and then late in 6:6, with a form of the same word, it correspondingly states that God came to a decision "after *profound deliberation*."

The two verses, one after the other, contrasted, with this word variation, the purposes of the thinking process. In the first, humanity was being described as misapplying its gift of intellect by possessing a non-profound course of thought, which was entirely one of wrongdoing. Then in the next verse, as apart from humanity's misuse, there is the implication that God instead was more appropriately using intellect through a more thorough deliberative manner, that of examining a worldwide situation.

The same term again for thought, *dianeuó*, was also employed at the end of the flood at that verse 8:21, where God, impressed by Noah's sacrifices at the newly-built altar, was correspondingly *giving thought* to the fate of humanity:

> 8:21) "In *giving thought*,
> I will not compound the condemnation"

Verse 8:21, in going on, demonstrated the contradiction of the thoughts of human beings with a term associated with *dianeuó*, by the use of the related word *dianoia*, containing a hint of antipathy toward misapplied thought, here as "notions":

> "While the *notions* of human beings
> Still incline toward
> The wrongdoing of youth"

In antiquity, there was the long-held view that the heart, rather than the brain, was the center for thought, and for the emotions. The term for the *heart* (Hebrew *leb*, Greek *kardia*) was recurrently adjoined in scripture with

27

derivations of words for thought, and at times toward misdirected or youthful emotional thinking.

Much later in the Bible, there was a corresponding word combination, to redirect humanity's thoughts back toward the right path, in a prayer from King David to the Lord, containing several of the words earlier appearing in 6:5 and 8:21. There, at *1 Chronicles 29:18*, the terms for intentions, thoughts, heart (Hebrew *yetser, machashabah, leb*) were positioned one after the other, phrased as: "In the imagination of the thoughts of the heart" (KJV). In Greek, those three words in that latter verse may appear now more literally clinical, as they are: Intentions/imagination (*plasma*), thoughts (*dianoia*), and heart (*kardia*), together providing an aggregate for the concept of the heart-oriented view of thinking.

Returning to the third of the first three verses, at 6:7, and to the thought processes of God, it concludes with:

"This,
The result of my decision
To have brought them
Into being."

From early times, these authoritative words in this ending passage of 6:7 have regularly been translated as the expression of sorrowful emotion, stating that God *regretted* or *repented* or was *sorry* for creating humanity. In Hebrew, for that, is the verb *nacham*, and in Greek is the longer alliterative verb *metamelomai*. While each can indicate a meaning of repentance, sorrow, or regret, each of these verbs of emphasis also possesses an explicit meaning of a *change of mind*, to alter a concern to one which would lead to a positive state of betterment. The term *metamelomai*, separated into its two root components, *metá (after with*, or *change afterward*) and then *melō* (to *give thought*, to be *concerned*) when merged together imply a resolution, a redefining of purpose, but not exclusively one of sorrow.

Either ancient term provides the inference that after considerable thought, the process itself has yielded a pronounced analytical revision. With "This, the result of my decision" there is a subtle subtext of regret.

In a down to earth manner, to use a commonplace example of the basics of this verse, one might envision a modern authority figure, one in an albeit more limited realm, regarding a prior project seen as no longer sustainable, stating words to the effect of: *I've seen enough of this, it's time to put a stop to it, and get back to basics.*

An ancient orator could have adopted comparable authoritative voicing during this early portion of the recitation to correspond to that, using spoken words to underscore an all-inclusive point. On a vastly enlarged front, the entire world was here described as being re-thought, and was about to be revamped, in these opening verses.

5

The Early Verses

After the very first three verses of the narrative, the succeeding three-verse passage returns to the third-person narrator's words. They indicate that God registered approval of Noah, who was an exception, unlike that immediately prior, which referenced humanity in general. This description begins at Genesis 6:8:

> 6:8) However,
> One
> Had attained the approval
> Of the Lord God.
> 9) There was Noah.
> Noah:
> Righteous,
> A man of integrity
> Among the others of his time,
> Highly regarded by God.
> 10) Noah,
> A father of three sons,

Named: Shem, Ham, and Japheth.

These three verses provide a brief but definitive description of the character of Noah. Verse 8 is concise: "However, one had attained the approval of the Lord God." Verse 9 begins with wording that for centuries often has stated: *This is the account of Noah*, or *these are the generations of Noah*. That one word, *account/generations* (in Hebrew *toledoth*, in Greek *genesis*) implied reference to an individual as a part of a once-living family record, a declaration of one's life.

Its Greek root (*gen*) followed later in the same verse. Phrased there often as *in his generation*, it again implies living within those of that same generation or *time*. Here, first, "There was Noah" expresses that in a similarly succinct manner, and the succeeding phrasing, "among the others of his time" identifies his distinction in manner of contemporaneous living.

Between that wording, the verse contains a compact synopsis of the character traits of Noah, that he was a righteous man of integrity. In the ancient phrasing, in Greek the proper name Noah is succeeded by three illustrative modifying terms, or, listing all four: *Noe, anthrópos, dikaios*, and *teleios*. In English they literally are: 'Noah, man, righteous, integrity.'

To look at each: First, after the name Noah (which in ancient Greek was written Νὼε), there is listed *anthrópos* (written ἀνθρωπος), here meaning *a man*, in the singular. Plural forms of the word (such as people or humanity) were used earlier in verses 6:5-7, for human beings, to distinguish from other living beings. *Anthrópos* is the root word for the field of study, modern *anthropology*.

That term is succeeded by *dikaios* (*dik´-ah-yos*, or δίκαιος), meaning righteous, dutiful, virtuous, impartial, and implies a high level of piousness (in Hebrew, *sedeqah*, of the *just*), one who entirely fulfills obligations.

Finally there is *teleios* (*tel´-i-os*, or τέλειος), meaning one of fully-formed maturity, of a completeness of character, of integrity. *Teleios* through its root can suggest a connection to the centuries-old hand-held tube-shaped *telescope* (*tele-scope*, or Greek combination: *complete viewing*), which when extended out segment by segment, could be completely focused and function at a fully realized magnification and strength. These last two terms together (*dikaios* and *teleios*) imply self-realization, a wholeness in mode of living.

The verse concludes with: "Highly regarded by God" and in Greek, "highly regarded" was *euaresteó* (*yoo-ar-es-teh´-o*, written ενηρέστησε), meaning pleasing, to serve well, to have conduct acceptable to, to be in high regard, and which was placed adjacent to *Theos*, God, as written in actual Greek lettering in the verse: θεώ.

While no knowledge by the reader of Greek script is in any way required here, merely by actually viewing how these words would have looked in print, with literal translation below them, may nonetheless assist in understanding the phrasing by actually 'seeing' the terms in their word order.

How they would have been resoundingly spoken aloud, in the paced, and paused, intonation of an orator in those times, with sections even sung, can add to their ancient impact through observing how English transcription has been determined. The two segments, as written in Greek, with English beneath each, are:

Νώε ἀνθρωπος δίκαιος τέλειος
Noah man   righteous integrity

τω θεώ ενηρέστησε Νώε
to God regarded-was Noah

In the above, the first line begins and the concluding line ends with Νώε, Noah, demonstrating that even within small sectors, mirroring by emphasis was prevalent. In the second Greek line above, the central verb, ενηρέστησε, or *euaresteó*, *pleasing* or *regarded-was*, in Hebrew was *halak*, meaning followed or walked in the path of, as in having gained full acceptance by God. The translated verse's finalized ending phrase of "highly regarded by God" is also a reemphasis of the prior verse's "attained the approval of the Lord God." It comprises a repetition within the two back-to-back verses of 6:8 and 6:9. Verse 6:10 concludes the short segment with the names of Noah's three sons.

The wording in the unified three verses of 8, 9, and 10 places Noah as one in the ways of God, and by kinship it also places his family as differentiated from the rest of otherwise corrupted humanity.

The effect of these brief sentences was to contrast Noah, and the high regard for Noah, significantly with the description in the three verses coming before, which described the hostility within the others.

Also, in like manner, after the three-verse description of Noah, the next three-verse segment returns again to humanity's wrongs. Summarizing composition from the very beginning for the first nine verses displays the three-fold format:

> God saw wrongfulness (verses 5-7)
> God saw Noah, an exception (8-10)
> God saw wrongfulness (11-13)

The first and third sections, three verses before and three after Noah's character synopsis, each describe wrongdoing and unrighteousness, and in the same format: They both begin with two verses of (third-person) narration of what God had observed, and then are followed by a third verse in God's quoted words. This third section is again in the three verse form of:

> 1) Narrator's words (about the problem)
> 2) Narrator's words (about the problem)

3) God speaks (about the solution)

This (longer) segment of 6:11-13, in that configuration is:

> 6:11) But still,
> In the very sight of God,
> Desecration
> Was engulfing the world,
> Deceit,
> Overtaking the world.
> 12) The Lord God
> Was witnessing
> The earth's regions
> Approaching ruin.
> The one correct course
> Was being utterly abandoned
> By the many,
> Those living and breathing,
> All across the lands.
> 13) And it was then,
> The Lord God
> Disclosed to Noah:
> "A breaking point
> For human beings
> Has been reached
> Here before me.
> It is certain that,
> Spreading from them,
> The earth
> Is being severely defiled.
> Now, listen well:
> I bring an end to this,
> To the world as it is."

The wording within the third verse of the first section, at 6:7 ("I am about to sweep aside") is expressed again in the wording of the third verse of this third section, 6:13 ("I bring an end to this.")

Looking at the beginning verse of this sequence, 6:11, it speaks of "Desecration" and "Deceit." The ancient phrasing for those two segments consists in part of two verbs which have often been translated as *was corrupt* and *was filled*. In both Hebrew and Greek they are paired, as each sounded similar to one another in those languages. In Hebrew they were *shachath* and *mala*. In Greek they were *phtheirō* and *plethō* (spelled εωθὰρη and επλήσθη) and in each the terms for "the world" (η γη) were also listed twice. Viewing the two segments in Greek can better demonstrate their repetition:

εωθὰρη   δε   η   γη
Was-corrupt yet the world

επλήσθη   η   γη   ἀδικία
was-filled the world deceit

In Greek, earlier in 6:9 the term "righteous," *dikaios*, to denote Noah, was in 6:11 contrasted by using its opposite, that final word *adikia*, unrighteousness, or "deceit." The basics of this verse 6:11, observing the problem, are substantially repeated, in coinciding but slightly varying wording, in the next verse, 6:12, which again is:

6:12) The Lord God
Was witnessing
The earth's regions
Approaching ruin.
The one correct course
Was being
Utterly abandoned
By the many,
Those living and breathing,

All across the lands.

Each verse begins with God's observations, at 6:11 with: "In the very sight of God" and equivalently at 6:12 with: "The Lord God was witnessing." Each verse mentions forms of negativity, at 6:11 with "desecration" and "deceit," and 6:12 with "ruin" and being "abandoned." Then each concludes with the extensiveness over the earth, at 6:11 with "overtaking the world" and 6:12 with "All across the lands."

Proceeding again to the final verse of this entire nine-verse opening sequence, 6:13, it addresses the onset of the forthcoming first critical juncture, the coming catastrophe, as the first words of God to be spoken to Noah, and in the first person: "A breaking point for human beings has been reached here before me." In the King James Version, following closely the earlier Geneva version, for the same phrase, it is stated: "The end of all flesh is come before me." (The Geneva version called it "*an* end" rather than "*the* end.")

In Hebrew, for *end*, the word *qêts* (pronounced *kates*) referred to the end (usually of time) or to a furthest border. In Greek, the word for this endpoint was *kairos* (*ka-hee-ros'*), a term meaning a fixed time or due measure. In Psalms 119:96 the word was used in: "I have seen an end of all perfection" (Geneva and KJV).

In each example, there is a meaning of an upcoming limit, a culmination, an end-point, or in contemporary terms, "a breaking point" comparatively can now suggest that approaching of a critical, calamitous threshold of reckoning.

Also in 6:13, one small connecting term, an easily understated conjunction which linked two adjoining phrases, bears examining, as it demonstrates that a return to a more ancient type of interpretation can add intensity and clarity. The Hebrew word *ki* and Greek *hoti* have both usually been translated as simply *for* or *because*. The original word served to affix two statements in the verse. It was, paraphrasing: The breaking point had been reached *'because'* of the people who were severely defiling the world.

The word *because* can still be applied as a workable connector there, however in antiquity it had a more broad definition, one coinciding with what could be visibly seen, more as: *Evidently,* or *For this reason,* or *Doubtless.* The term served to not simply connect, but to allow the latter phrasing to unmistakably provide the observable reason for the earlier wording. To use, instead of *because,* as God speaks, "It is certain" supports a more significant conjoining emphasis, with "It is certain that, spreading from them, the earth is being severely defiled."

These verses 6:12 and 6:13 also reference "by those" and "from them" which serve as a contrast with the exception, the one being spoken to, Noah. The wording (pronouns in Hebrew and Greek) served to separate Noah as one who, while part of humanity, had been described as not behaving in the negative manner characterizing people as a whole, the many who were acting woefully as a group entity.

Within the initial nine-verse segment of 6:5-13, the wording for the sum total of *the world* and its surface appears regularly, for example, once in each of the first three verses. To describe the earth's surface, the word in Hebrew was *erets* (*eh´-rets*) and in Greek was *gé* (*gh-yee´*, written either as: γη or γης). In both languages, each is synonymous with terms for world, earth, territories, regions, surroundings, the land surface.

In English *gé* has become the common prefix *geo* where it has been combined to form such world-related words as *geo*logy and *geo*graphy. The use of Hebrew *erets* or Greek *gé* is very prevalent, appearing in over half of the verses of the narrative, and often multiple times within the same verse.

But in modern English, repeating one word, such as *world* or *earth* time and again may not resound with equal impact among contemporary readers, especially since the modern mindset of *the earth* is conventionally one of the round orbiting planet, conveying far different imagery in minds of today.

The perception of those times was instead commonly toward a flat earth, and the terms *erets* or *gé* long ago alluded to the solid ground, to the regionally soil based lands and in some contexts could include the adjacent seas. To only use *the world* or *the earth* repeatedly or exclusively now would create for readers a different mental picture than was originally conveyed. As such, going back to vocabulary which more closely elicits the far earlier cultural experience better transmits this representation, bringing nearer what the scriptural text was relaying to its audience of those times. Moreover, the term as used in those times carried an additional impression of the earth as being an arena, a theater, as in, now, a theater of operations, the enlarged world for all to inhabit.

Therefore, rather than solely restating *the earth*, the more ground-based wording has been used in some phrasing for the term *erets* or *gé*, to more effectively establish what those listeners at that time would have been easily envisioning, to express the concept of their world in language understandable to readers now.

Within the three verses 11 through 13, relating again to the wrongfulness of humanity, there the terms *erets* or *gé* originally appeared twice in each verse, or six times in that segment alone. As used here, the first verse of the three, 6:11, does repeat the term *the world*, and then at 6:12, for expression of terrain, the grounding words *earth's regions* and *the lands* secure the segment's central placement. Verse 6:13 then uses *the earth* and *the world as it is* once each. For the two verses 6:11-12, to clarify, each usage is emphasized:

6:11) Desecration
Was engulfing *the world,*
Deceit,
Overtaking *the world.*
12) The Lord God
Was witnessing
The earth's regions
Approaching ruin …
All across *the lands.*

It can be walking a translational tightrope to apply synonyms for one expression, or for one extensive concept, especially with a traditional turn of phrase, just as, in the opposite, earlier translators had in other circumstances in this same narrative employed only one word for multiple scriptural terms. Words exist to depict images, and a translator's goal is to concisely and accurately represent the imagery which informed the original listeners by presenting those same concepts in current like-minded expression. It is vitally important to primarily, and as clearly as possible, express those perceptions which had come easily into the minds of listeners of that past time with the appropriate terms which will just as easily convey those same perceptions today.

Thus, as their view of the earth was different from that of today, and it was, then analogous words need foremost to reflect their earlier view, and only after succeeding at that can the universality and timelessness of the original message again begin to properly come through. To convey those thought forms in today's readily recognizable words is the translator's ultimate purpose.

To emphasize that ground-based world concept, as the narrative progresses the appearance of *the earth* twice in one later verse at 6:17 is a part of a continuation of the initial remarks to Noah. The verse also contrasts *water* (Hebrew *mayim*, Greek *hudór*) and *the sky* (Hebrew *shamayim,*

Greek *ouranos*) with the two usages of *the earth*:

> 6:17) "A flood of *water*
> Onto *the earth*,
> To lay waste
> To all beings
> Which take in
> Their breath of life
> From beneath *the sky*.
> As many as there are
> Upon *the earth*,
> Each shall meet an early end."

This verse contains the contrast of *the earth* with what can be perceived as *non-earth*, or what is other than land surface. First, it mentions *water* and then *the earth*, then upward to *the sky* and back down to ground level, *the earth*.

In other connecting and contrasting circumstances one chapter later, there are three successive verses, 7:17-19, which emphasize the drastic inundation of the entire world with the floodwaters. Within each verse, there are contrasts between the *non-land*, that is, either *the waters*, or *the heavens* above, and their being in discordance with the disappearing lands in between, reflecting a back and forth, or up and down diverging association. With those contrasts of excessive water, features of land, and heavens, the three verses are:

> 7:17) *The waters* advanced,
> Uplifting the Ark,
> Elevating it
> High above *the surroundings*.
> 18) The unrestricted *overflow*,
> Ranged ever further,
> Inundating *the lands*,
> Carrying the Ark
> Upon *its waves*.

19) *The waters,*
Seemingly without end,
Concealed *the expanses,*
Overspreading every one
Of *the mountains*
Under *the heavens.*

In the first of these three, 7:17, the contrast is between *the waters* and *the surroundings.* Also, in between them, that same verse possesses a successive placement of raising of height on each of three lines, with *uplifting, elevating,* and *high above.* Proceeding to the next verse, 7:18, another word trio, this of variance, begins with the *overflow* and to *the lands* and then back to *the waves.* In the third of the three verses, at 7:19, it is a balancing of *the waters* with *the expanses* and then upward to *the mountains* and still higher to *the heavens.* Word formulations such as these serve to accent the ongoing intensity of the unfolding inundation.

For another, and still later example in the next chapter, during the lessening time of the flood, the usage of the world's surface and water are twice matched in the same verse, at 8:13:

8:13) *The water* had receded
From more of *the world* ...
Water was lowering
Over the face of *the earth.*

As through the words of an orator, to accentuate extensiveness, the broad-based nature of the deluge was being heavily stressed, with frequent comparisons and contrasts.

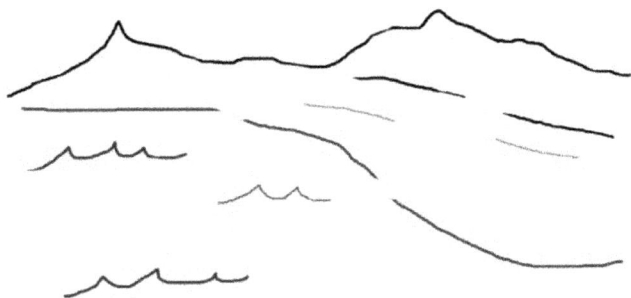

6

Building the Ark

AT THE VERY OUTSET of the narrative, the ancient texts state that God surveyed wrongfulness (6:5-7), saw Noah as an exception (6:8-10) and then returned to further address the wrongfulness in humanity (6:11-13) in three verses each. That final verse, 6:13, contains "A breaking point for human beings begins here" and then "I bring an end to them," possessing wording of both a beginning and an ending. The verse also functions in a transitional manner, by setting the stage for the next three verses, which are instructions on what is to be built, and they each individually continue in the three-fold, trinary format..

So, after the initial nine verses, the next three verses (14-16) sustain the system of composition, and each of these verses possesses its own internal threefold styling. They are each commands to Noah on how to construct the craft (the term for "Ark" appears twice in each verse) and constitute the description of its classical features.

These instructions include the outer and inner framework, and provide the dimensions and additional attributes in an ordered progression. The verses describe:

14: The outside hull, the inside structuring, and coating for inside and outside.
15: The scale: Its length, width, upcoming height.
16: The finishing features: Assembling it upward, adding a door, and three floor levels.

Those three verses, extended lyrically to reassert the orated format, are:

6:14) "For this reason
You, yourself
Will be building
An Ark.
Begin with
Squared timbers of wood.
Bind together beams
To be aligned
Within the Ark,
And seal
With securing veneer
What will be
The inside and out.
15) You shall then
Lay out the Ark
To this:
Five hundred feet
The length of the Ark,
Eighty feet its width,
Fifty feet
To be its height.
16) To join together the Ark:
You will raise it,
And closely connect it
At its crowning point.
Also, a door

You shall install
In the side
Of the Ark.
And with
A ground floor,
A second floor,
And a third,
You shall
Make it ready."

The sequence begins and ends with the two directives of "building an Ark" and "Make it ready." With two additional verses, one before and one after this segment (6:13 and 6:17), there is more mirroring, as the three central building verses are situated between the two surrounding boundary verses. Both with 6:13 directly before and 6:17 following after, each of those two bookending verses states that God is preparing to lay waste to the world. They are:

6:13) "Now, listen well:
I bring an end to this,
To the world as it is."

And then, after the 'how to' build the Ark:

6:17) "As many as there are
Upon the earth,
Each shall meet an early end."

These two surrounding verses serve to set focus upon the three-verse informational building sequence within, which are the details on how to construct the Ark.

Also the concluding verse at 6:17 is followed by another longer instructional segment starting at 6:18, which begins with God's lasting Agreement with Noah, and 6:17 thereby functions additionally in bridging to that, which leads to the further specifics for Noah, those listing the animals then designated to be later arriving.

The instructions, as with all the instructions until late in the account (which at that point included his sons), were here being stated to only Noah and to no one else. As verbal presentation, they were being heard in words plainly understood by the audience.

Examining the how-to terms of 6:14, early in the segment there is: "You, yourself will be building an Ark." The verb form *to build* in Hebrew, *asah*, has been customarily translated in English as to '*make.*' *Asah* is more generally defined as *to do* or make something, to bring about, or to prepare. In Greek, it was *poieó* (*poy-eh´-o*), a verb with a variety of subtle distinctions, often also basically defined as *to do* and *to make*, but in its many usages carried much more meaning. It meant to fabricate, to make ready, to manufacture, and even to create. It appears throughout the narrative in several nuanced forms, for example, in verse 6:6 *poieó* is used there as *create* ("God reflected on having *created* people.")

Later, and back to 6:14, the historically common choice of the term '*make*' has been translated here with an equally uncomplicated yet updated word: "*Building* an Ark." The reason is that, in ordinary speech, it typically is not now said that one is to *make* a house or a ship, but instead, in light of proportion, it is much more common to say one is to be *built*. The largest edifices now are called *buildings*, and today there are homebuilders and shipbuilders, as *build* in those descriptions is self-evident.

Saying to *make* such a craft now would imply a smaller item, such as a model or prototype. While this one verb clarification may seem rather minor, using forms of *build* can help return a proper emphasis to the greater magnitude and structural framing aspects which were in this segment, back then, easily recognized.

For a task today, perhaps one can envision a somewhat

comparable down-to-earth example in an understandable modern format. If instructions were coming, in a building-trades style, from a top-notch architect, a designer, or an owner, and were being conferred upon a hired contractor, who was receiving unique specifics on how to assemble one monumental, far from ordinary craft, then those numerous instructions may be seen as presented, in oratory, one after another, in a relatable approach.

To make explicit these particular instructions now perhaps more colloquially, and here in an 'owner to contractor' manner, what was expressed as being said to Noah essentially was: *'Here is how I expect you to build this'* and then what follows are the very direct requirements about its essentials.

Looking at the original scriptural wording for the keyword 'Ark,' it was envisioned by ancient listeners differently than common current impressions, as the term used in those times was not specifically or necessarily applicable to a boat or water vessel, but was to be more generally understood then as a type of secure box.

There is no mention of a type of boat or floating raft/barge in the flood narrative, as there were other words which could have been used for those. The Hebrew word used for Noah's craft throughout is *tebah*, meaning a type of enclosed container which is applied to only one other item in the entire scripture, and that was in the next book of the Bible, the book of Exodus - and the same term *tebah* was used there to describe the 'basket of the bulrushes' of baby Moses.

The author of the initial books of the Bible has been traditionally referenced as the Prophet and lawgiver Moses, and that author, as with any individual or any chronicler, described objects and events from within the cultural framework of their own times.

That latter bulrush episode in Exodus tells of how, to hide the infant Moses in Egypt, he was placed by his mother into a modified basket and left at the banks of the river, and was then discovered at the shore by the Pharaoh's daughter's retinue, wherein he was rescued and then raised in the royal household. The descriptive verse is:

> And when she could not longer hide him, she took for him an ark of bulrushes, and daubed it with slime and with pitch, and put the child therein; and she laid it in the flags [reeds] by the river's brink. (Exodus 2:3, KJV)

It is worthy of note that Moses or his scribes, as author, would use this unique word, a *tebah*, and only in these two instances, first for that of Noah and, for another episode centuries later, for that of Moses' own infancy. In that latter verse, it states that the mother of Moses took a conventional basket (ark of bulrushes), one for carrying, and then waterproofed it, creating for it a new task: To allow it to be buoyant in water. That item, a *tebah*, whether the largely wooden chest of the Great Flood, or the small basket of durable papyrus reeds, in each circumstance referred to an object with an outside shell and a top covering that was then converted to be made watertight.

This alteration, the application of waterproofing, would have been understandable to listeners of that era, as this type of item, of conventional regional material, was described as having been repurposed, given a refashioned flotation role.

By applying the same word to both a very large made-to-float type of chest as well as to a converted household basket, their connectedness would have been totally reasonable within the times, as each would have designated a corresponding type of receptacle. Each was made of known components, each was described as sealed, modified to carry its passenger or passengers for a special lifesaving function. The dual connection would have been sensibly synonymous an author who had been brought up in Egypt at a time when items of those basic compositions were in everyday use.

Sharing the same term, a primary difference then between the vessel of Noah and for the much later item, the adapted bulrush basket of the infant Moses, is one of capacity: The first was huge, and the second was proportionately small. As for their respective tasks, that was the same: To be made to float, and to act as a protective artifice for their very valuable contents.

Therefore to better define *tebah* in more current parlance and sharing those likenesses, one could use now a more common designation, such as each being a lifesaving craft, or a modern all-weather enclosed lifeboat. As with many rescue craft, neither biblical *tebah* had any of the traditional accessories of a boat: No rudder, no steering or guidance mechanism, no oars, no mast, and no sails. For either the one of Noah or of Moses, it would only drift, and just rise and fall with the water level.

Moving back exclusively to the very large vessel of Noah, it was, as described, in many ways at its most basic, to be a huge sealed barn built atop a barge. It required no direction, or to be taken to a specific location. As with any emergency craft, it was not designed for multiple usages, it only had to keep afloat, and just once. Modern translations of Noah's *tebah* in other languages have used related and appropriately utilitarian wording to describe it. In current Spanish, for example: *una casa flotante* or *a floating house* has been used as one of the Biblical equivalencies, instead of the word *Ark*.

As terminology has changed, now where large scale shipping is routine, and huge seagoing vessels are commonplace, the variations between a boat and a reed basket, different even in those times, are even more pronounced now. While a wooden floating vessel and a modified child's basket could be seen in that long past era as sharing features, and could be accorded the same word, that parallel currently is far less easily grasped. Their differences, not their likenesses, are more recognizable to people now routinely knowledgeable of large ships, and hand-held baskets are more likely to be perceived as only rarely used or as antiquated decorative items.

Two different words are usually listed for today's Bible readers, and from the earliest versions, two words were used as being more understandable. In Greek the word for Noah's vessel was *kibótos*, a wooden box or chest. But for the basket of Moses, in Greek there was a different word, *thibis*, basket of papyrus, rather than a re-use of *kibótos*. More centuries later, the Latin Vulgate translation of the Bible maintained that tradition, for the phrase *arcam de lignis* (chest of wood) was used to characterize the Noah vessel, and again a separate Latin term *fiscellam*, basket, described the basket of bulrushes.

In Latin though, *arcam*, or ark, was also applied to a separate, third type of container, the Ark of the Covenant, which was also called Ark of the Testimony, the chest which carried the Ten Commandments. As with the basket of Moses, it is also described in the Book of Exodus. In Latin, the same phrase *arcam de lignis* was used for that somewhat different type of container. That sacred chest was represented in Hebrew with the word *arown*. A rectangular wooden box, covered in gold, with two gold rings projecting from each side, it was designed to be transported using long poles inserted through the side rings. *Arown* (or *aron*), also was defined as *box*, an enclosed chest, or in other contexts, it was used in reference also to a coffin or a crate.

In English the use of 'ark' for all three of these objects came about through the adaptation of the terms from these earlier works, primarily by way of the Latin root word. So one word, ark, eventually came, directly and indirectly, to delineate all three objects, leading to the large barge-like vessel, the small floating basket, and the box of the testimony each being called an 'Ark.'

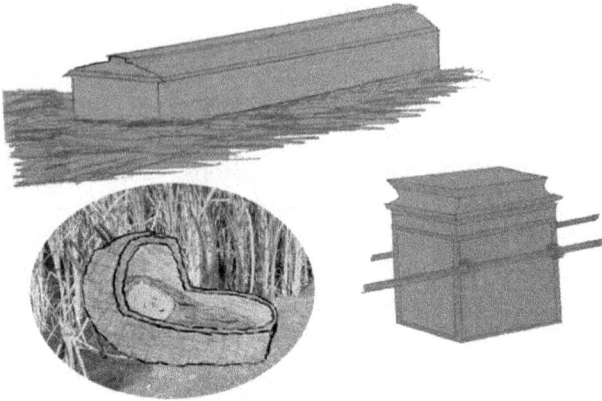

Each has been called "Ark" in English

The word ark by the 1400s was used in English both as a boat and as a cabinet, so that one word would have been understandable to those within that more recent era. Ark to denote all three objects was consistent with using today the comparable word *container*, as in a transportable container, as there are now modern container ships, and for baby Moses, a small floating container, and for the sacred testimony, a land-based box or container. It is not uncommon that when translating different but related words for the newer language to use one word, especially if there are not clear differentiating synonyms. The term ark more conventionally applied to these items centuries ago, and was suitable for the earlier English speakers. Each of these, the watercraft, the basket, and the chest, is an enclosed container, they share in common the conceptualization of protection, and in each of the three biblical definitions they refer more so to that which was protecting what is sacrosanct.

But Ark in recent English only primarily refers to two usages, either to the vessel of Noah or to the chest of the Testimony (the Ark of the Covenant), as it no longer has any other everyday modern referents. As mentioned, the basket of Moses is normally referred to now, as in earlier times, as simply that, a basket.

To return to just the vessel of Noah, while the more modern words lifeboat, or rescuer, or even a barge (with a barn, as a zoo, atop) may each be somewhat of an adequate equivalent, none alone today can fully match the originally enumerated impression.

For practical understanding, Ark in English is so well known and culturally so tied to the craft of Noah that it is simply not easily replaceable. The word Ark as used primarily for the large watercraft of the Great Flood still readily applies, it easily calls to mind a strong visual impression, still effectively conveying the early concept as an immense floating vessel, and so it is used here.

Moving forward in the wording, in verse 6:14, after "building an Ark," next comes: "Begin with squared timbers of wood." In Greek it was: *ek xulon tetragonos* as *ek* meant *from* or out of, *xulon* is *trunk of tree*, or wood, and *tetragonos* is squared, or four cornered; so the phrase carries meaning of *wood, four cornered* or of *timber, squared*. However, going back to that small preposition *ek*, while *from* or *of* is a simple translation, the word actually had a 'two-layered' meaning, as in 'out of here to there' or 'a first step,' and to use phrasing now to convey a type of command, as to initiate from a certain point of origin, "Begin with" can better get that brief point across, and especially to more accurately depict the forceful wording, especially if portrayed by an orator with reference to the imparting of instructions.

Next, to *xulon tetragonos*, that wording did not designate a unique type or species of tree, but instead, for the raw building material, it articulated how the timber was to be shaped, in the historic yet still conventional process in which round tree trunks are cut into a squared shape to be used as planks for framing. That understandable usage held forth for well over a thousand and a half years in Western Christendom, and it remains unchanged in the

Eastern Orthodox Biblical canon.

Maintaining that very early and plainly-expressed wording, centuries later, the Vulgate version of the Bible phrased it in Latin as *de lignis levigatis*, that is: *of timber planks*, of planed or smoothed wood. Still more centuries later, in earlier English form, the 1395 Wycliffe Bible continued that connotation as shaped timber for a watercraft, by writing: "Make thou to thee a schip [*ship*] of trees hewun [*hewn*] and planed."

In woodworking, hewing is the process of using an ax or other cutting tool to perform the task of chopping a log from its natural curved form into right-angled lumber planks, and a plane is a handheld trowel-like woodworking tool used to smooth the wood further. To hew and to plane were more difficult and involved tasks than the mere splitting of cordwood for kindling, which creates shortened, rough, and non-uniform cuts. Hewn timbers required more work, and were more expensive in time or cost.

But, in definition, over a century after the Wycliffe version's release, an interpretational change in English came about, referencing the term as it appeared in by then more widely available Hebrew Masoretic texts. In Hebrew the keywords are *ets gofer* or *trees, gofer*. The term *gofer* (pronounced *go fair* or in ancient times with a softer 'g' sound, as *zhoe fair* or *joe fair*) is written only once in the entire Bible, in this verse, and is recorded nowhere else, neither in Hebrew or allied languages. In such a circumstance, when there is an isolated word, and no other context to which it can be referred, it is called in linguistics a *hapax legomenon*, from Greek meaning *said only once*. Often shortened to a *hapax*, in philology any hapax can invariably be a problem, for if there is insufficient information to fully determine what that word means, it renders any type of definitive translation more difficult.

Preceding the Hebrew word *gofer* was the word *ets* (*ates*) and it can be translated as either *wood* or *timber*, or as the plural *trees*, as with the Greek. In the King James Version, early in Genesis *ets* is consistently translated as tree, for example it is used for the tree of life: "and a flaming sword which turned every way, to keep the way of the tree of life" (Gen 3:24, KJV). The 1534 edition of William Tyndale translated *ets gofer* as a particular type of tree, calling it *pyne* (pine) tree: "Make the [thee] an arcke of pyne tree" and the Geneva Bible also used pine tree.

The later King James Version, and many thereafter, instead chose to leave the Hebrew term *gofer* simply untranslated, and so it was written as 'gopher' transliterated phonetically in the method by which it was, by that later time, pronounced. Since then, *ets gofer* has more often been designated as a type of tree, by using pine, and also as cypress or cedar, given that they were used as craft building woods and remain indigenous to the region. *Ets gofer* has in English been additionally proposed to mean other types of tree species, especially as resinous woods were widely used in the King James era, the early sixteenth century, for selected wood types specific to the rising significance of shipbuilding. The German word *kiefer*, similarly sounding, refers to a resinous tree, a pine with needle-like foliage.

However, irrespective of choice, and whether the Hebrew or Greek term functions as the chief constituent, in either ancient language the expression defines the Ark, as per the instruction, to be decidedly constructed of wood.

Proceeding to the middle phrasing of this three-fold verse, it states: "Bind together beams to be within the Ark." It is here that what was to be the Ark's inner structuring was first mentioned, and here again the original wording has through the ages been interpreted by multiple designations.

The Hebrew word for these items was *qinnim*, a plural of the singular *qen* (pronounced *kane*). A form of that word shows up thirteen times in the Bible, but only in this verse and in no other was it used in the plural, thereafter making this definition also difficult. In the singular, when *qen* was translated the other twelve later times it was invariably called *nest*, as in a bird's nest, or symbolically, for a strong home. For example: "Strong is thy dwelling place, and thou puttest thy nest in a rock" (Numbers 24:21, KJV). In Greek, the term was *nossia*, again literally meaning nests.

Much later in the Old Testament, within the Book of Habakkuk, a three-verse segment uses *qen/nossia* in the first verse, and for wood, *ets/xulon* in the third verse. In this segment, the prophet Habakkuk was relaying a statement by God, quoted, as in the Ark segments, in the first person. The topic is of condemnation of powerful wicked individuals, and within the severe warning, the term 'nest' is used, then the wording emblematically refers to the setup of their 'house,' be it their dwelling place or their lineage:

> "That he may set his nest on high, that he may be delivered from the power of evil!
> "Thou hast consulted shame to thy house by cutting off many people, and hast sinned against thy soul.
> "For the stone shall cry out of the wall, and the beam out of the timber shall answer it."
> (Habakkuk 2:9-11, KJV)

Here, for 'set his nest on high,' the original wording, in both Hebrew and Greek, used terms meaning 'to arrange the height of his nest,' alluding to a forming and fastening, to a placement beyond conventional reach.

Following two verses later, the parallel 'beam out of the timber' phrase maintained this. In Hebrew, 'beam' was the word *kaphis*, literally rafter. The phrase, coupled with 'timber' (*ets*) has been often translated here as wooden boards that support a roof. As a whole, the three verse segment can provide insight into how those words were implying, in a then-recognizable manner, that which was in those times being seen as typifying secured reinforcement, to provide an overall strengthening.

The verse of Genesis 6:14, about the Ark, was written to also relate the particulars of setting up strengthening features. However, centuries after the Hebrew and Greek writings, Latin editions substantially modified the term for *qinnim/nossia* in 6:14 by then, as a phrase, using: *mansiunculas in arca facies*, or *rooms in the ark you build*. This somewhat altered interpretation, stated as types of rooms, was, more centuries later, maintained in English versions, for example in the Geneva Bible with "thou shalt make cabines [*cabins*] in the Arke" and in the King James Version (original spelling) with: "roomes shalt thou make in the arke." Original nested features, or even rafters, are not what are thought of now, as rooms. The use of the word rooms for this no longer fully captures the situating of framing that otherwise the ancient wording had suggested.

As a resolution, by further examining the ancient language, non-scriptural usages can additionally assist in discerning a return to a more forthright meaning. In Hebrew, in those earlier times, the plural *qinnim* was translated not exclusively as nests, but instead more broadly as larger nest materials, as sturdy *reeds* or heavier *stalks*. In watercraft of the era, *qinnim* were lashed together for strength, and on land they were bound together for similar objectives, as inner frames to fabricate supporting columns, and likewise, for other uses, they were purposed as thinner staffs or staves.

Viewing the plural of this word to be for a type of tightly fettered robust configuration, it allows the phrasing to remain consistent with that labor intensive wood-cut forming, the wood timbers which came immediately before, in the same verse. Rather than as individual compartments for hatchlings, to return to the application of *qinnim* as a type of *beams*, each bound together, used for framing, adds appreciable clarification. As with square cut timbers to form an outer hull encasement at the start of the verse, so for inner fabrication, where support is supplied by strongly-bound ribs at the ceiling level, and where interior stabilizing joists would attach to an inside hull.

By using *beams* in the midpoint of this verse, with the term listed immediately *after* the squared timbers, and *before* the inner and outer sealant, it can, as was better understood at the time, more closely demonstrate that the entire verse possesses a unifying theme, one of creating impressive high-quality durability inside and out.

In Hebrew, the term *qinnim* was accompanied by *asah* (make or bind), then the preposition *eth* (in, beside, together with), and then *tebah*, Ark, or, literally: Place bound beams within the Ark.

In Greek it was first *nossia*, then *poieó* (make or bind together) with the preposition *katá* (*throughout*, within, also repeating at 7:14 for the entering of species *down from* or *by* their type) then *kibótos*, the Ark, again regarding an ordered or aligned placement within the framework.

In a spoken sense, in Greek, the word *nossia* actually flowed well, having been situated among the multi-syllable pacing of the wording within the verse. With the terms of *poieó, seautou* (you), *kibótos*, the word *nossia* conformed, as fitted within that larger context.

The Hebrew term *qinnim* can be still better understood by viewing not only the surrounding phrases in this same verse, but also with the two verses following, as they further allude first to inspiring scale at 6:15 and then to internal differentiated horizontal levels, to the three floors at 6:16. In a warehouse sized structure, individualized rooms can ordinarily be assembled during or after floors were built, after the framing itself was situated. In such buildings today, the room arrangements and sizes can be easily changed, depending upon the tenant's needs, without altering the framework. Also, the animals to be within the Ark are not mentioned until 6:19 with: "Where you are to guide them." Thus the broader term *beams* in 6:14, five verses before, suggests a more valid architectural step, one taking place early in the overall process.

The consistency of this verse is about structuring, about building solidity, inside and out. If the inside *qinnim/nossia* were to be conceived of as rooms, or compartments, or as cubicles, then current thoughts will be redirected largely toward those, and toward housing their future contents, an important topic, but not the one being immediately addressed.

Here, the verse subject was the intactness of the Ark itself, and on how that Ark was to be envisaged, to be created as an enormous well-composed object of firm framing. If the Ark was to be unmistakably seen as to be built to embrace and sustain a remaining world, then that priority should, as originally in this portion of the instructions, remain upon the basics of the foundational edifice, the only element under discussion, the structure itself, and of its solidly understood design. By so doing, the tri-fold unity of this verse remains predominant.

To that end, with a return to an interpretation of supportive beams, a more majestic subtext of meaning can be found underlying the term. Ornately woven *qinnim* staffs were displayed long ago as symbolic of power and influence, carried aloft by individuals leading in processions and shown in other formal functions. Even in the modern era, a bejeweled staff held by enthroned monarchy continues to serve as representation of royal authority. The word *beams* in English carries a double meaning of both wooden boards and *(beams of)* light, and using that word in the central section of this verse can not only refer to the basic inner strengthening of the craft, but, as it had in times past, can again suggest an inspiring preeminence.

Moving to the third of the three phrases in this one,

once-plainly understood verse, the final wording of 6:14 is:

> And seal with securing veneer
> What will be
> The inside and out.

The first two sections of this verse concerned first the "squared timbers of wood" (plural), and then secondly the "beams" (also plural). This third portion of phrasing again refers to the same items, this time to their "inside and out" sections. At its most literal, this phrase addressed the requirement to add a wood treatment, to surface the planks and beams with a top-notch, for the times, type of liquid-like substance which would later harden to provide waterproofing and durability, and also would, through the higher quality and method of administering those ingredients, at the same time impart an impression of sanctity.

The wording "securing veneer" describes an ancient concept, that of wood finishing from tree resins, to be used as a layered coating. In those times, one term for a valuable imported substance, lacquer, originated from the Indian language Sanskrit. There the term *laksha* referred to an adhesive, obtained from insects on certain trees, which was used for a better and more rare type of coating for surfaces. It was transported, along with valuable wood, to the Middle East and then further west.

For centuries, English translations of this section of verse 6:14 have twice here used the term *pitch* ("and shalt pitch it within and without with pitch" Geneva and KJV) or a form of tar, a natural substance used as a blacktop or asphalt, to cover or seal.

In Hebrew the two terms for pitch were actually separate words, first *kaphar* and then *kopher*. Looking again to Exodus 2:3 and the basket of the bulrushes, with the phrase "daubed it with slime and with pitch" (Geneva and KJV), there the original Hebrew word later also called pitch was *zepheth*, a substance which would liquefy in the sun. All three terms had been called 'pitch.'

Here at Genesis verse 6:14, with the phrasing in Greek, two forms of the word 'asphalt,' or *asphaltos*, both as a verb and a noun, were used. It first employed *asphaltos* in the verb form, as in to *apply* asphalt, or basically *you shall asphalt* and then following, after *inside and outside*, it enlisted the same word in noun form, as *with asphalt*. Also in Greek however, those word forms meant *securing*, or to safeguard, a sense of *to lock in*.

Returning to Hebrew in this verse, two separate forms were engaged, but as mentioned, from two entirely different yet similarly sounding words; the verb *kaphar* and then the noun *kopher*.

The first, *kaphar*, referred to ceremonial sacrifice, that of covering the sacred altar of the temple, and with an affiliated meaning of: To *appease*, to atone or make amends, to be cleansed or purged of sins. For example, *kaphar* was termed *atonement*, regarding sacrifice at the altar: "for this blood shall make an atonement for the soul" (Leviticus 17:11, Geneva Bible). The verb *kaphar* carried a meaning of bringing about an atonement for prior wrongs, through an anointment.

Returning to verse 6:14, *kaphar* was then paired with a different word, *kopher*. *Kopher* can be defined as a rare veneer, a sealant of plant derivative, but it too carried an additional meaning, in fact its primary meaning, that is, as a valuable sum of money, such as a fee to pay for a dispensation, or an amount of a bribe to safeguard a life. In the next appearance of the term, in Exodus 21:30, it is stated as a *ransom:* "If there be laid on him a sum of money, then he shall give for the ransom of his life whatsoever is laid upon him" (KJV). That word, *kopher*, more specifically regarding wood treatment suggests both the functional property of a high-end sealant and, through such an item of value, the fostering of *protection*.

Kaphar and *kopher* each, in a related manner, referred to salvation-defining ointment-type covering. In their time, the contrast between the two individual words, the more noteworthy atonement-oriented *kaphar* set against a tree-based sound-alike *kopher* would have been an understandable yet divergent association for the describing of two processes, one being sacrificially sanctifying and the other the adding of a more material, but nonetheless expensive, protective.

Looking back, for this wording, John Wycliffe's 1395 version did utilize the two-purposed interpretation. His wording for this in 6:14 was: "and thou shalt anoint it with pitch within and withoutforth" and this imparted both first the adding of an *anointing* and the use of a *pitch* sealant. It afforded an appreciation of the contrast and duality of the two separate but balancing words.

To simply use words today to the effect of *seal it with a sealant* or *cover it with pitch* wouldn't quite capture that additional meaning of the two separate words. Used here, "seal with securing veneer" applies a compatible style to convey the pairing of the two complimentary yet still reinforcing terms.

Returning to the Hebrew word used earlier in the verse, the tree term *gofer* could be seen as originally bridging phonetically to the phrasing ending the verse, to the two words *kaphar* and then *kopher*, connecting the early term with those two ending the verse. The three terms possessed a harmonious sound, and also had related meanings, for as a timber correlative *gofer* was used to build, and *kaphar* and *kopher* to seal with the wood-originated anointing substance. The pronunciation of the three words would have been lyrically evident to the ancient listeners.

To paraphrase this one verse, 6:14, it was originally saying: *You will form this container from well-cut wood, and inside, position finely-crafted beams, and for both inside and outside, you are to use ceremonial-quality sealant for its strengthening.*

Collectively, what was being described would have served to insure the listeners that the product, of better workmanship and materials, was to have been not only sturdy but also was, in a manner, to be consecrated, giving it a depiction of holiness.

For readers today, possibly more accustomed to updated variations of the terms *gopher wood, rooms,* and *pitch,* the use here of *squared timbers, beams,* and *veneer* might constitute a significant shift. It is a shift backward, as the focus of this work has been to return to words of original clarity, to their primary expressions of meaning. For a verse describing the formative materials of the Ark, this older style wording remains in compliance with those ancient fundamentals.

In the original, this verse traversed the Ark, it flowed in its 'Out-In/In-Out' description with: First the outer wood hull, then second the inner beams, and next, the inner and outer coating. That allied type of threefold listing is maintained in the following two verses, 6:15 and 16, to be clarified in the next two chapters, as each of those verses is also descriptive of the Ark by matching means.

7

Defining the Ark's Dimensions

MOVING TO THE NEXT verse, of more instructions, this specifies the three exterior dimensions of the Ark:

6:15) You shall then
Lay out the Ark
To this:
Five hundred feet
The length of the Ark,
Eighty feet its width,
Fifty feet
To be its height.

This lists the outer measurements of the Ark: Its length, width, and height, in the current designation of feet. The ancient wording used the term *cubits* and rather than 500 feet, 80 feet, and 50 feet, stated the dimensions (equally rounded and equally diminishing) as: 300, 50, and 30 cubits.

The cubit, pronounced *kyoo-bit* and a common unit

measure of length from long ago, was based on a very human characteristic, the length of a forearm from the back of the elbow forward to the long middle fingertip of the outstretched hand. It was readily available for one needing to make a rapid estimate, and it functioned as a handy increment midway between the length of a now-standard foot and the three-foot yard until well into the modern era.

The Hebrew word for cubit is *ammah* (*am-maw´*), derived from the expression for *mother*, as in *mother unit* of measure, and also a meaning for *forearm*, or together: *mother unit of the arm*. That phonetic coordination with *mother* remains common throughout many languages: мама in Russian, *mère* in French, *madre* in Italian and Spanish. In Greek, it was *péchus*, also meaning *forearm*. Related, the Egyptian hieroglyph for cubit was a symbol for the forearm, with the palm facing down:

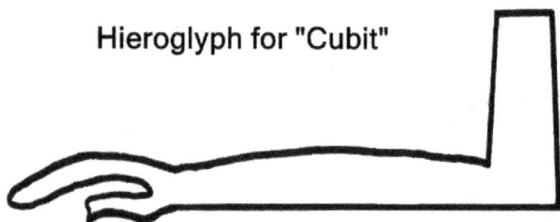

Hieroglyph for "Cubit"

Cubit in English is derived from the Latin word *cubitum*, meaning *elbow*. In the Middle East of that time, the cubit was in frequent use, but as a standard it did have regional variations. Inevitably, as larger construction projects came about, greater precision was required. What was often practically selected was the forearm length of an important personage, to be then used for major assignments. Over time, those units were maintained, often for centuries.

The Egyptians utilized a dual set of cubits, a longer or royal cubit, around 20.6 inches, and the common cubit, around 18 inches. That slightly shorter common cubit was used less formally, but because of its easy availability (a characteristic adult hand-forearm length) it nonetheless became a staple within the field of building.

The longer, more official, Royal Egyptian cubit was used in the construction of the Great Pyramid, and of those versions, cubit rods from that era still exist. Very closely confirming that same size was another cubit measuring rod from the Babylonian era, rediscovered in the twentieth century.

In 1916, during World War I, the curator of the Archeological Museum in Istanbul, Turkey, identified a copper alloy object of 518.6mm, or 20.41 inches, already in their collection, as a cubit measuring rod from Nippur, in now modern Iraq. At approximately one half of the modern meter, and from over four thousand years ago, it varies only slightly from the Royal Egyptian cubit.

Nippur Cubit Replica

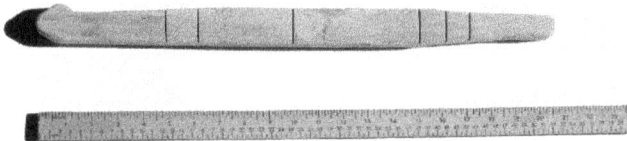

Using either the Royal or Nippur measure, 300 cubits would place the Ark's length at a little over 500 feet, while using the shorter common cubit places it at a little less than 500 feet. That is about a modern football field and a half in length, and a 50 cubit width, using the same field comparison, is narrow, at slightly over half a football field's width. The dimensions for ancient listeners, and now, were of an extremely long and narrow rectangular shape, with easily memorable rounded numbers.

The back-then mainstream measuring rod, and its

resemblance to one's hand and lower arm, can in themselves function as a microcosm for visualizing the shaped appearance of the Ark, to which a speaker could easily have referred when engaging the cubit concept.

With a long boxlike description, this length to width proportion (300 to 50, or 6 to 1) would have presented an oversized but feasible image to those acquainted with watercraft, as that ratio is still common for non-motorized vessels, as with envisioning the length/width of a canoe or kayak, or seeing the long shape of a barge with shipping containers. The Ark as specified would have been about half the length of an average modern container ship.

From the instructions, that extremely large 'box' for the time suggested holding capacity rather than of streamlining to maneuver the waves. The floor space of each of the three inside floors of the Ark (mentioned in the next verse) and using the Nippur cubit length, would equal a current acre (43,560 square feet), a substantial inside area, and vast for listeners of the times.

The term *cubit* was used in three verses in the Flood episode, first in 6:15 and 6:16, describing the Ark's construction, and then later at 7:20, to acknowledge the maximum height of the waters, there originally stated as 15 cubits (or half the 30 cubit Ark height) above the highest mountain peaks.

Finding a precise modern synonym or equivalent for *cubit* and still retaining rounded parallels to those 300-50-30 numbers can be difficult for translators, as proportionately it has now been replaced by measures either smaller or longer, with no single common unit now that exact size. A *half-yard* or *half-meter* can seem unwieldy when converting to larger multiples of numbers. In Spanish, some modern translations do use *codo*, meaning elbow, the half meter, to update that biblical standard.

With feet, a popular designation currently in translation is the use of 450-75-45 feet, but that diminishes the cubit length, and the rounding is lost. To quickly conceptualize those measures now does not necessarily come easily to many individuals.

A use of the metric system in this verse has also at times involved somewhat awkward conversions, for instead of 300 cubits for the length, shifting it to something near 150 meters could retain accuracy, and also would require halving the width and height numerals, down to near 25 and 15 meters. Some translations do use such conversions, even proceeding to decimals, but those modifications again lose the impact of the rounded scriptural numbers.

Those diminishing round amounts: 300, 50, and 30 had a proportional bearing to both skilled artisans and general listeners of that era (300 to 30 is ten to 1, 300 to 50 is six to 1, and 50 to 30 is 1.6 to 1). Now altering them to meters or to other present-day number ranges can significantly change them in modern visualizations, thereby distorting today's reader's perspectives, taking away the once easily-perceived designations. The numbers of the narrative: 300, 50, and 30 cubits, could be readily apprehended at the time.

Here, briefly dropping more-modern zeros from 300-50-30, that initial 3-5-3 ratio in ancient architecture was common, using then specifications derived from the 'Golden Mean,' which was long seen as an ideal proportion, both in building and as a standard of beauty in art. That Golden Mean has been later characterized by the Greek letter Phi (written Φ), and numerically expressed by 1.6, now more specifically as 1.618. For the 3-5-3 ratio, it is equivalently 1-1.6-1 when reduced proportionately to smaller numbers.

There are still existing examples from that distant era of the knowledge and use of a '1 to 1.6 to 1' correlation in design attributes, such as again Egypt's Great Pyramid (its base to height ratio), and various dimensions of the Greek Parthenon (rectangular breadth as well as the layout of column arrangement).

The cubit average (halfway between the royal and

common cubit, or 19 modern inches) is 1.6 times longer than the present-day foot. This connection to the past now has enabled here a rather simple solution, a conversion process from cubits to the dimension of feet, one which keeps the numbers rounded, as in antiquity.

To help explain, a short list of a simple number concept (dating from ancient times, and now known as the *Fibonacci sequence*) can demonstrate this *then-to-now* association. Here are six small numbers, the first two of which repeat, then begin to increase: 1-1-2-3-5-8.

As a number chain, each integer in the brief listing is the total of the previous two numbers. Beginning with the first number, 1, and adding it to the next number, also 1, their sum equals the third number, 2. Then, the 2, added to its prior number, 1, equals the next number, 3. Each equals the sum of the prior two numbers. Continuing, 5 equals the prior 2 and 3, and 8 equals the prior 3 and 5, as the numbers grow.

What is applicable here is that each ascending number, after the 2, will always be 1.6 times greater (the Golden Mean) than the prior smaller number, no matter how high they continue. In that long-past era, there were many who were aware of this type of geometric sequencing, which when applied in building was seen to yield very favorable structural and visual results.

Here, to use the list to explain the conversion from the cubit average into modern feet, again the series is: 1-1-2-3-5-8.

Simply advancing in the latter part of that number sequence one digit up, proceeding from a back-and-forth '3-5-3' next up to '5-8-5' allows for an easy and accurate adjustment (and reinstating the more modern zeros) from 300-50-30 cubits up to 500-80-50 feet. The ratio between the 3s and the 5 is essentially the same as that between the 5s and the 8 (each being 1 to 1.6) and retains those same descending round-number and rectangular proportions of the original 300-50-30 cubits.

With 500-80-50 feet, and half the final 50 foot Ark height, that is, the water depth of 25 feet (15 cubits) above the mountain peaks, all are now in observance with the receding Biblical numbers. There is an understandable numerical calibration, a modern tape measure which preserves the close succession of that 1-1.6-1 (and 3-5-3 and 5-8-5) association, furnishing a faithful portrayal of the originally connoted Ark scale.

For listeners of that time, hearing of the vessel's huge size, a cubit was a contemporary and convenient sizing. Using the foot, or plural term *feet*, can help carry that understanding forward, and more easily, to modern readers. Of the Ark dimensions, taking only the third and first, the 50 foot height and the 500 foot length (30 cubits and 300 cubits), with the length ten times longer than the height, it is an easy reference to conceiving of the size being described, in terms comparable to those of antiquity.

Also, for the building process, this verse ends with: "Fifty feet *to be* its height." The use of "to be" is consistent with the future tense used in these verses, and correlates to the incremental steps of the process, which will be described in this book's next chapter (The Top, the Door, the Floors) as the height is to occur last, with the Ark's sides to be uplifted.

The primary benchmark of *cubit* transfers with it an archaic implication, but once understood, with its *elbow to fingertip* length, and by using modern wording, the bygone measures can once again be more effectively envisioned. The ancients would have heard them expressed in oration, and in those times, through a presenter's accompanying broad gestures, with distant lengths being shown as spanning away, as down a nearby field, those features could have been imparted in grand manner, vocally and visually.

8

The Top, the Door, the Floors

THE FOLLOWING VERSE, the third of the three 'construction' verses, begins with:

> 6:16) To join together the Ark:
> You will raise it,
> And closely connect it
> At its crowning point.

Over the centuries there has been disparity as to how these words, comprising the initial section of verse 6:16, are to be correctly interpreted, especially as there is again a difference between the Hebrew and Greek wording. In Greek, the phrasing began with three short components, which, paraphrasing, said: To join (*the sides of*) the Ark together, you will need to raise (*each of them*), and then connect (*each of them together*) at the top.

By displaying the wording in Greek and English, that opening terminology of 6:16 and how it rather glided together can be better shown literally. The word *episunagó*, written επισυνάγων and meaning *joining*, begins the verse, and the segment closes with *from above*:

επισυνάγων	Joining (together)
ποιήσεις	raise/create-you-shall
τον κιβωτόν	the ark
και εις πήχυν	and by cubit
συντελέσεις	complete-you-shall
αυτήν άνωθεν	this from-above

Looking at it more closely, in Greek, there is first that verb *episunagó* and it is defined as: To narrow, to *join* or collect together. In other contexts, that versatile verb was used in describing the gathering together of crowds of people, to create a large assembly at one location. Here the verb is in participle form, meaning *joining* or in *order to join*.

In a building setting, for the describing of how to put together one enormous framework, the *joining* or gathering together refers to the step of narrowing, a tapering leading in an upward angle to the rooftop, to a suggesting of a pointed obelisk-like shaping, traditional to the time.

The term *episunagó* was followed (on the next of the listed lines above) by *poieó* (written ποιήσεις), the frequently used and also multi-functional verb (three times in this full verse alone) with slightly varying meanings (all allied to assembling, to artistic creation, or to production of completed appearance) depending upon context. For example, a few verses earlier, at the beginning of the narrative in 6:6 and 6:7, there were three usages of *poieó*, each affiliated with creating, as: "Having *created* people," then "humanity, those I have *formed*," and third, "*brought them into being*."

The same adaptable word *poieó* was applied in each of the two verses immediately preceding 6:16, there in the instructions to *build*, to *bind*, and to *lay out*. Within these verses (6:14-16) on how to form the Ark, *poieó* itself, appearing six times in just these three verses, with multiple connotations, helped to define each of the fabrication steps, first with *building* (and then *bind* beams) in 6:14, then to *lay out* the sides, initially laid out on the ground according to their assigned dimensions at 6:15, then here at 6:16 with *raising* those sides.

It more specifically in this context referred to the procedure of *raising up*, as in an old-style barn raising.

The two verses prior, 6:14 and 6:15, can be thought of as the act of constructing the framing two dimensionally, that is, on the ground, adjacent to also constructed over-the-ground base flooring.

In 6:15, the length and width of the Ark, starting as flooring, are listed first, then came the 50 foot, or 30 cubit, height ("Fifty feet *to be* its height") which will be reached when raised in sequence. It was a quite common building practice, in both ancient and even in modern times, wherein the frames, the sections, are fabricated, laid out, and partially sealed while essentially on their sides.

What occurs then, from that placement, with the bases situated and remaining at ground level, the out facing sides, as here at 6:16, are actually uplifted, by humans or harnessed animals, often with pulleys and ropes. The sections could be moved upward from horizontal to vertical, with the top portions being attached to upright beams and then connected at an angle, forming a peak. This would achieve a final narrowing, a sloped configuration.

For this description, commonplace and flexible words of that past time were used, and would have been readily understandable to those then, who would have often seen buildings, animal barns, and small homes ordinarily assembled in this manner. In modern times, unless similarly practical terms are used, the now nearly obsolete 'barn-raising' concept can be lost when in print. An orator, with arm and hand movements, could more easily demonstrate the concept.

For this onset of 6:16, in Greek the actual four-word

phrasing again that opened with *episunagó* (to join) is followed by *poieó tov kibótos* (you-shall raise the ark) to describe that beginning of the uplifting process.

Next the terms are somewhat more involved, with *kai eis péchus* (and by cubit) followed by *sunteleó* (written συντελέσεις), meaning to *complete*, to *bring to an end point*, or to *connect together*. *Sunteleó* contains the same root as *teleios* in 6:9, which described the maturity and completeness of Noah. Thus here, to open this verse, three verbs: *episunagó*, *poieó*, and then *sunteleó* align to conceptualize how to *join*, to *raise* and to *connect* the framing of the Ark, to its uppermost portion.

In English, for the 'and by cubit' wording, a literal 'foot and a half' sounds odd as a contemporary term, and doesn't now carry the more colloquial original reference, which was of the woodworking specifications for bridging interlocking rafters at a roof's peak. Today it is better illustrated, and still briefly, with "closely connect it."

One might now visualize that orator, while speaking commandingly, with arms forward, moving the forearms and hands upward and then interlocking the outstretched fingers, to smoothly represent the steeple-like beam connecting process.

The section of text then ends with *outos anóthen* (written αυτήν άνωθεν) meaning *this from above* or *this from on high*, it also meant *from heaven*. Later in Genesis, the same word *anóthen* was used for *from above* at 27:39: "and of the dew of heaven from above" (KJV). Here, "crowning point" possesses, in a more contemporary manner, that same type of high-up, elevated 'capping off' of an angled rooftop.

Also later in this same verse, the multi-use verb *poieó* appears twice more, next referring to the instruction to *install* a door, and finally was used in concluding the verse by the firmly stated "You shall *make it ready*" as would be understood when coming from a superior.

While each of those practicalities could be easily channeled in those times with one well-used and readily tractable word, repeating that one verb (Hebrew *asah*, Greek *poieó*) now with a far less specific term like 'shape' or 'make' at each instance would leave modern readers puzzled, even perhaps wondering at what to 'make' of such unclear instructions. Thus the need now for the focused wordings bringing back the subtle yet distinctive aspects of a process which was once easily expounded.

As for look and sound, then and now, viewing simply the Greek (end of line) suffixes, (such as 'ɛις' or you-shall), along with the prevalence of the letter *'pi'* (the π) and its 'p' sound (*epi*-sunagó, *p*-oieó, and for cubit, *p*-échus) then the phonetic compatibilities of that wording can in a way be seen, or otherwise, perhaps even heard.

The terms were saying, in rather euphonious phrasing, that by joining together through tapering, by lifting the sections toward the top, then the roof portion, and the entire frame of the Ark, is to be closely (within a cubit) aligned, up toward the heavens.

Skipping momentarily to a few verses later, to 6:21, and related to the opening verb, *episunagó*, there is a shared verb form. That verse is:

> 6:21) All types of food to eat.
> *Collect it together,*
> To sustain yourself
> And each of them.

In Greek, the verb in 6:21 for *collect it together* is *sunagó*, containing the same root as *episunagó*, and used there as to *accumulate* for safekeeping. Each of the usages of the two verbs implies the concept of putting together, in the first as narrowing the framing together to join for a rooftop, and in the second to collect food together for storage.

In Hebrew, to return to the same top-shaping terminology of 6:16, one particular word has often come across quite differently in translation. The Hebrew word used, a noun, is *tsohar* (*tso´-har*), defined as *midday*. As phrased, the verse literally begins with: 'A *tsohar* shall you make for the *tebah* [Ark].' *Tsohar* in its *singular* form shows up only in the Bible in this verse, in reverse of the one-time plural usage of *qinnim* (beams) two verses before it. When used each time afterwards in the Bible, *tsohar* is plural, causing the defining of the singular word in this verse, especially over the millennia, to be more difficult. The plural in other later verses was used as *noontimes*, or midday. As an example from further along in the Bible: "And it came to pass, when midday was past, and they prophesied until the time of the offering of the evening sacrifice" (1 Kings 18:29, KJV).

In this later instance the plural of *tsohar* is used as a time of day, possessing an implication of when the sun is at the highest. But, for its use in the singular in Genesis 6:16, for a top portion of the Ark, a strict time of day for a vessel completion fitting would be less contextually valid, so it had been at times suggested instead to have been meant for lighting, given the meaning of brightest time of day to let in sunlight, or as an air opening or a *window*.

The term for *window* has often come about in translation for *tsohar* in this verse, having first been used in Latin. In the Latin Vulgate window (*fenestram*) was applied, as shown with the opening phrasing of this same verse in Latin and English:

fenestram	window
in arca facies	in ark make
et in cubito	and in cubit
consummabis	finish
summitatem	at-summit

Following that Latin interpretation, the translations of Wycliffe, Tyndale, Geneva, and King James versions each also used *window*.

In that verse, and elsewhere within the flood narrative,

in earlier English the word *window* as mentioned became a common default term for several phrasings. It had also been adopted in the succeeding Genesis chapters 7 and 8 as the entirely separate *windows* of heaven (rather than as it is called here: "*towering enclosures* holding oceans above the skies") and also later in chapter 8 for the *window* of the Ark that Noah opened to first release the raven. Hebrew and Greek employed separate words for each of those three instances.

To differentiate, the *tsohar* in 6:16 has in more recent centuries been interpreted not just as a *window*, but as a type of skylight or ventilation opening. Additionally, regarding accoutrements to the top of the vessel, to the barn-like upper portion, variations in translation have also extended to it referring to such potential items as eaves or gutters, or to a turret type wall on top of the roof, around its upper periphery to redirect water over the sides, as well as to any type of small but long opening at the top. However, by returning to the more definite Greek meanings of *episunagó*, to join together, with *poieó*, to raise, and *sunteleó*, to connect, they continue to fulfill the logic of securing the wooden components of the Ark at its peak.

In Hebrew, looking beyond that one word *tsohar* to the wording coming after it, were *tebah* (Ark), *ammah* (cubit), then *kalah*, meaning to bring to an end, to finish, or fulfil, and *maal*, meaning from above, upward, higher. This opening wording of the verse, in addition to describing the higher portion, was written rhythmically, with the phrase endings in Hebrew following *tsohar* being: *Tebah, ammah, kalah, maal*; and all associated in sound. But the same words often used in English versions: *Ark, cubit, finish, above* do not sound nearly as much alike, so readers in translation will in some versions be denied the complimentary lyricism that the early words possessed.

Transliterated from Hebrew, the wording can reclaim a bit of how the words were originally presented. Here is a segment of the phrasing, with phonetic Hebrew and with

English:

lat-tê-bāh	for the ark
wə-'el-	and within
am-māh	(a) cubit
tə-ka-len-nāh	shall you finish
mil-ma'-lāh	from above

Each of the lines above contains either a short *a* (the āh) or a *schwa* (short e) sound (or both), providing a clipped and well-paced lyricism.

Here the modern adaptation, through alliteration, "closely connect it at its crowning point" can assist, also through a type of cadence, in recapturing some of that styling.

To return to the full wording of this involved verse:

> 6:16) To join together the Ark:
> You will raise it,
> And closely connect it,
> At its crowning point.
> Also, a door
> You shall install
> In the side of the Ark.
> And with
> A ground floor,
> A second floor,
> And a third,
> You shall
> Make it ready.

This verse, as with the each of the two immediately preceding it, traverses the Ark. The description encircles the vessel, moving around it, beginning first with the elevating of sides and connecting above, and it then proceeds to one side, with a door, and then continues inside to three internal levels. By this crisscrossing, the wording provides another overview, giving the readers or listeners a more vivid image of the forthcoming Ark's contours.

As for the second and third segments of the verse, those which refer to the side door and the three levels, they are less subject to terminological controversy. The original Hebrew word, *pethach* (*peh´-thakh*), is defined as an opening, doorway, an entrance, as was the Greek word, *thura*. Fortunately, door, irrespective of language, has a clear meaning. Situating a door in the side of a box-like vessel is imminently understandable for the loading of any type of cargo.

Here for installing the door, the Hebrew verb *sum* (*soom*) was used, meaning to set, or to make/install, and is akin to *asah*, to make, a form of which also was applied later in the verse. In Greek, the verb again is *poieó*, here "install" and it will appear a third time in the verse, for "Make it ready."

Back to Hebrew, adjacent to *sum* in the phrase, the term *tsad*, which means side, was used, and is equivalent to *side* in English. This description of the door on the side, applicable for specific use on this vessel, was utilized here, but *door* was not named anywhere else in the same episode. The Ark was described as having been sealed by God, and without repeating the word for door. In the next chapter at 7:16 it states: "And then the Lord God shut the Ark from the outside" with no door specifically mentioned. Then again, in chapter 8, with both 8:16: "Proceed forth, out from the Ark" and 8:18: "And emerged Noah and his wife," no door was specified.

In the scripture three *levels* within the Ark were implied, and the first Hebrew word *tachti*, (for lower, or at the foot of) rather than first is used, which then is followed by the ordinal numbers for *second* and *third*. In Hebrew this was rhythmic, as each was pronounced with an emphasis upon the final syllable:

> Lower: Tachti (*takh-tee´*)
> Second: Sheni (*shay-nee´*)
> Third: Shelishi (*shel-ee-shee´*)

Their commonality produced a natural lyricism, more so than do those of their English equivalents, as *ground, second, and third* can only attempt to replicate that linguistic balance by using an even meter. Additionally, an actual separate accompanying word for *levels* or *decks* or *stories* is not in the original, and has to be subsequently placed in other languages by implication, as a designation after the scriptural words for ground, second, and third. In Greek they were written, and rhyming, as: *katayaia* (from the ground), *diorofa* (second floor), and *triorofa* (third floor). In the Latin Vulgate it was phrased as *latere deorsum cenacula et tristega* or *downwards* (lower), *middle, and third* (floors).

The Wycliffe Bible (1395) translated it as: "Thou shalt make solars and places of three chambers in the ship." *Solars* were the private chambers or staterooms in a medieval English house. Later, in the Tyndale Bible (1534), it was translated as: "And thou shalt make it with three lofts one above another." There *lofts* was used, with *loft* referring to an upper chamber, and in those times would reference an attic type area. The Geneva Bible (1560) used *room*: "Thou shalt make it with the low, second, and third room." For contemporary phrasing, using *floor* in English can allow for a more clarifying designation, and still is able to provide repetition conforming with the scriptural pacing, as here: "A ground floor, a second floor, and a third."

Three Verses of Three

The expressions within the three construction verses

have described:

14) The outside hull material, the internal frame, and the inside and outside coating
15) The scale to which the timbers are applied: length, width, height
16) The features - the raised framing, the side door, and the three interior floors

Each of the Ark's essentials stressed eminence, that this vessel was to be out of the ordinary, and was to serve a high purpose. There were hints of grandeur throughout all three descriptive verses, implying that this was to be different, as if a temple construction were being assigned.

It had for ancient listeners, as in verse 14, the well-formulated material, it was to be huge as in verse 15, and in verse 16 it was equipped with additional sizable features, including the multi-floor interior. Along with some recognizably commonplace wording, mixed within its to-the-point phrasing was the subtext that with this vessel, there was more. This vessel, this event, was special, and within the description, it was being expounded as one of a kind.

In this translation, by mixing somewhat now-archaic wording (you *shall*, and some subject-verb reversals) with aspects of current speech, there has been the effort to retain and to replicate the original verbal structuring. As mentioned, the phrasing of the verses here, as in the scriptural text, starting with "Building an Ark" and with similar phrasing to conclude the third verse, the decisive "Make it ready" matches the arrangement of antiquity. Following the scriptura, each of these three verses maintains their internal threefold format, and each retains the succinct command-like style, given that these were written as integral instructions to be followed.

9

The Affirmation

AFTER THE INSTRUCTION ON how to build
the Ark, then came the first specific mention of an
upcoming flood. The next verse, 6:17, states:

6:17) "Know this:
I will be inflicting
A flood of water
Onto the earth,
To lay waste
To all beings
Which take in
Their breath of life
From beneath the sky."

Then, immediately following that, an exception was
being made, a reassurance to Noah, with a "lasting
Agreement." At 6:18, it is:

6:18) "Yet, as to you,
I put forward

> This lasting Agreement:
> You will be permitted
> To stay within that Ark."

That Agreement could be considered as a type of decree from God, and also as an avowal, a guarantee to Noah. What comes next is a listing of all those to enter the Ark, specifically first Noah's family, to be followed by the various animals to be safeguarded. Much later, after the effective departure of those on the Ark, there came the expression of completion (the rainbow) of the fulfilled guarantee.

At 6:18, this vital wording of a type of an Agreement was readily recognized in ancient times, as is comparably now the issuance of an executive order, or, when between individuals, the signing of a contract. In both Hebrew and Greek, it was expressed in just a few words, but it had a culturally well-defined impact.

In a time of Kings, the issuance of a royal decree, an imperial edict, was an order to be followed, directed to all subjects, or at times to one selected individual. Unlike a mutually consented person-to-person contract, such an order was unilateral. Nonetheless there were similarities, then as now, to what was a valid contract. An edict, as with a contract, could bestow benefits to both parties – a job completed for the leader or government, and also security or potential rewards for the vassal, the follower.

To examine the wording of 6:18, there is the key term for "put forward" which in Hebrew was *qum* (*koom*), defined as to arise, to stand up, and also to make binding, to appoint, to decree. In Greek the same term was *histémi*, written στήσω, also meaning to take a stand, or to set forth, to sustain with authority.

Later in Genesis, the word *qum/histémi* was phrased as *stood before*, when Joseph's brothers appeared before him, then Governor of Egypt, at Genesis 43:15:

And went down to Egypt, and stood before Joseph. (Geneva and KJV)

Affiliated with "put forward," the term for the "lasting Agreement" in Hebrew was *berith* (*ber-eeth´*), a treaty, an alliance, to be in league with another. While legally it could also be an ordinance issued by a monarch to their subjects, it meant, even more, a sacred or divine pledge, a guarantee.

In Greek that term was *diathèké* (*dee-ath-ay´-kay*), written διαθήκην, a frequent word in Greek legal papyri, meaning a valid binding arrangement, such as a will, as it was essentially a contract between two parties, usually face to face, there in the "here and now," often attested before others. In those times, it meant literally to take a public stand and then make a pledge with another. That phrasing of 6:18, in Greek, and with explanatory English, is:

και στήσω	Yet-now I-stand-forth
την διαθήκην	the agreement
μου προς σε	mine here-with you

That basic one-to-another concept continued in later centuries and translations, for in Latin the phrase was written: *ponamque foedus meum tecum*, or defined literally: *ponamque* (to form) *foedus* (in league) *meum tecum* (me with you) or: 'I will form in league with you.'

Advancing in time, the 1395 Wycliffe version used *covenant of peace*: "And I shall set my covenant of peace with thee." Later, the 1537 Tyndale version worded it as: "I will make my appointment with thee." Both the Geneva Bible (1560 edition) and King James Version (1611) returned to *covenant* and the phrasing: "But with thee will I establish my covenant."

In up-to-date speech, the words *establish* and *covenant* do not ordinarily occur together, even within formal legal terminology. That wording now can come across as cryptic and somber, rather than as it once was, easily comprehensible.

While now the one-word 'covenant' could be replaced with merely the word "agreement" alone, that does not nearly approach today the overriding and long term importance of what was being originally communicated. The terms, with their supporting clarifiers ("as to you," "This") produced an image of a profound long term, person-to-person legacy with enduring import. A sense of their inferred multi-generational quality is more unmistakable in another verse later in Genesis, 17:7, where, in speaking to Abraham, the word *covenant* appears twice, and God stated:

> Moreover, I will establish my covenant between me and thee and thy seed after thee in their generations, for an everlasting covenant, to be God unto thee, and to thy seed after thee. (Geneva Bible)

That generation to generation, life to life connotation, expressed now as a "lasting Agreement" comes closer to what was then quite obvious to ancient listeners, what was a type of fixed decree in those times.

Also, and less formally to those then, it was a not uncommon public model of two parties each pledging to perform separate tasks and to ultimately achieve and reinforce their respective ends of agreed upon assignments.

Now, looking at what could be viewed as legally on a similar level, in just a person-to-person variation to what those of long ago understood, and one type of more current comparable circumstance: If a modern property owner arranges terms for a new home to be built on their own land, an agreement (often with clear-cut and detailed requirements) can be made with a handpicked reputable contractor to construct the dwelling, with the landowner acknowledging to fully compensate the hired contractor for the new home upon its successful completion.

In this biblical episode, a contract of worldwide importance was being described. It was placed immediately after God's message that the entire earth was to be laid waste ("to lay waste to all beings") with the important exception of Noah and only those to accompany him. As it states, God was pledging, upon Noah's demonstrable accomplishment, to spare those specific lives.

But in the meantime Noah, for his end of the arrangement, as the 'contractor' of record, had a great deal of work ahead of him. Noah was assigned the demanding tasks of building the Ark to conform to expensive large-scale specifications, of gathering the necessary food, and of sustaining the assemblage of animals for the duration.

With this coming after the Ark building instructions, each of these three verses, 6:17-19, begins with a clear introduction: "Know this," "Yet, as to you," "Furthermore."

The third verse among those, 6:19, contains more of Noah's responsibilities, it continues with an expanding list, containing types of animals to be accommodated in the Ark. It states:

> 6:19) Furthermore ...
> From each of these,
> You are to guide them
> Into that Ark
> Where you are
> To provide for them,
> Male and female, alive,
> There,
> With you.

The wording here makes explicit Noah's delegated sphere of obligation. The verse contains the directive: "You are to *guide* them into that Ark." The verb, in Hebrew *bo* and Greek *eisagō*, is usually translated as *bring*, but that implies that Noah was to have earlier assembled the animals together. The verb has a primary meaning of to *come in*, or enter, or to be guided within.

For the final aspect of the phrasing of verse 6:19 are Noah's listed animal-care tasks, and most versions may not stress the definitive locational aspects, but instead use variations of: *To keep them alive with you, they are to be male and female.* In particular it has not been common at this point in the verse to use both the terms "Where" and "There."

The original wording of these lines was attuned unambiguously to the Ark. By being cared for at that location, within the Ark, which was to be created as a type of sustaining refuge or 'island' isolated in water, then it is better reinforced that those animals, and only those which were to be "there" were to fall under Noah's assignment. The wording possesses the attribute of their being alive and *right there* and to be cared for at that 'station,' the sole nexus of responsibility for Noah.

To delve more deeply into literal verse-ending wording, both the Greek and English are listed, in two segments:

ἱνα   τρέφης   μετά   σεαυτοῦ
Where you-feed with   yourself

ἀρσεν καὶ θήλυ   ἐσονται
male and female they-shall-be

The first of the two segments is saying in effect: *where you may feed/maintain* (them, or those animals) *there with you - yourself.*

The very first word, ἱνα, or *hina*, is defined as: *so that*, or *where*, or *in that place*. It reinforces the place where the animals are to be kept (the Ark to be built). The term carries a significance, not to be downplayed or even at times excluded, of meaning *in order that right there* Noah is to care for the animals, and the single word "Where" can fittingly fulfill that.

Continuing forward on that line, to τρέφης μετά σεαυτοῦ, or *trephó meta seautou* in western script, meaning *you take care of them*, and, and given that it was a first person to second person directive, it is making certain that 'you' (Noah) keep them fed.

For the second Greek line, the first three words, ἀρσεν και θῆλυ, or *arrén kai thálus*, are the terms *male and female*, and they are not, as often translated, the final terms of the phrase. Instead, the last word, ἐσονται, is a form of *eimi*, an encompassing Greek verb, for it is an expression of the multiple-meaning verb *to be*, or, for example in the third person plural: *They shall be, they exist*.

Here in this setting its usage goes beyond merely *to be*, but *to be living*, as it is about continuance of life, and also it is about a *discernment* of living, of continuing and existing at a *particular place*. It is relating a meaning that Noah must see to it that the animals under his care are to remain "alive" while "there with" him on the Ark.

This has been detailed in order to indicate that it was one of the major parts of Noah's *'contractual'* responsibility, a necessary portion of the agreement, the 'deal' being made and to be carried out, per specific instructions.

To further emphasize the importance of the animal protection aspect of 6:19, what comes next, the content of verse 20, is essentially a broad-based restating of 19, using only slightly different wording.

The first section of 6:19 is a listing of animals (both domesticated livestock and of the ground), and the first section of 6:20 is also a listing of more animals (birds, livestock again, and crawling animals of the wild).

Each of these two verses also possesses a very similar conclusion, about the necessity of caring for those to-be-gathered lives. Verse 6:19 ends by:

6:19) Two by two,
From each of these,

You are to guide them ...
Male and female, alive,
There,
With you.

Then verse 6:20 ends by:

6:20) Two by two,
From each of these,
Will be approaching,
There,
For you to take in,
Each male and female.

These two consecutive endings, if viewed again as long ago having occurred in performance, could be envisioned as close refrains, one after another, being echoed in the manner of a type of Greek chorus. In that setting, performing individuals who were positioned near to the orator added supporting emphasis to the orator's statements by means of intermittent repetition, lyrically interacting.

The next verse contains more instructions:

6:21) And you are to gather
All types of food to eat.
Collect it together,
To sustain yourself
And each of them.

The final verse of the chapter concludes with Noah's successful completion of those tasks assigned thus far, with:

6:22) What the Lord God
Had commanded of him,
He did accomplish.

The tasks for Noah will continue, as the next Biblical chapter, Genesis 7, lists more duties for Noah to fulfill. With the opening of that chapter, there has been the implicit passage of time, a beginning of a 'next Act' of the episode, and the Ark has now been built. The first two verses there are:

> 7:1) And then the Lord God
> Said to Noah:
> "You are to enter!
> You,
> And your entire family,
> Into the Ark,
> For under my observance:
> You
> Are of preeminent character
> In the midst of these times.
> 2) Now – To the clean livestock,
> Those,
> Which are pure for ritual,
> Those,
> You shall guide in."

In 7:1, the magisterial phrase "under my observance" appears, implying a high level of presence of perception, as it was in 6:11 with "in the very sight of God" and 6:13 with "here before me." Each of those verses contained the same wording, in Hebrew *panim*, meaning literally *face*, or adjacent to, and in Greek, *enantion egó*, or in the presence of me, in my eyes.

At 7:1, as elsewhere, God is issuing orders, and that authority, before one who is a dutiful subordinate, is made evident. The verse begins with praiseworthy remarks from God, with Noah described as "of preeminent character" and here it was granted that he was, with his family, to embark upon the lifesaving Ark.

But with the start of the next verse, at 7:2, an immediate

adjustment occurs, a solid reassertion of the 'owner to employed contractor' dynamic. The tone shifts, apparent at its start, with "Now – To the clean livestock."

With a deadline approaching, and as one might envision in a setting of command-like instructions and where direct clarity is essential, the commending, reinforcing words become, and here paraphrasing: *But enough of my compliments, let's get back down to business.*

As previously, Noah is given added workload, the list of duties goes on. There is a return to the basic, to-the-point details (a type of: *Pick up your tablet, more notes need to be taken*) about which, and how many, animals need to be cared for.

Just as earlier, at 6:18 where there was an affirmative attestation, the strong Agreement with Noah (and for his family): "I put forward this lasting Agreement" but then there was an immediate return to more instructions at 6:19. It began there with the words "Furthermore – From among all the beasts." For "furthermore," both Hebrew and Greek wording acknowledged the shift back to issuing added commands, moving from a focus upon Noah and his family and instead back to Noah's extended work duties, to that of preparing for the many animals to be joining him.

Separating 7:1 from 7:2, there is also this type of dispositional adjustment. The beginning wording at 7:2, returning to the animals, was achieved in similar manner (Hebrew *mik-kāl,* Greek *apo de*). In Greek, the two words, *apo de,* combined meant: *but apart from,* or *rather to this,* allowing the subject to shift. In current language, "Now" (followed by a dash) allows the direction to revert in like manner, to get the topic away from a brief commendation and to return to the immediate project at hand.

Transitions such as these can be difficult to make apparent in print. They could, in physical presence, be done more easily through an orator's gestures, changes in position on stage, or with a slight pause in vocalization.

Much later on, after the exiting of the Ark, and after Noah had successfully accomplished all of his assigned tasks, the Ark occupants were back on solid ground. At that point, at the time of 'payment,' it states that God then would expressly implement the completion of the earlier agreement, to compensate, to reward Noah and those with him, with an enduring pledge to thenceforth stand by not just Noah but all the living, to reassure that there will not be such an all-inclusive flood ever in the future. Using *promise* and *pledge* can convey that bringing to pass of the earlier statement, in contemporary yet still command-like and authoritative wording. Among the later expressions of this in Genesis chapter 9, in three successive alternate (odd-numbered) verses, are:

> 9:9) "Know this:
> I stand forth to uphold
> My promise made to you,
> And to your descendants
> After you,
> 10) And also to every living being
> After you."

> 9:11) "I shall stand by
> This promise to you:
> Never again shall all flesh cease
> From the water of the flood.
> Never again shall there be
> A flood of water
> To devastate the world."

> 9:13) "I unfurl my rainbow
> Among the clouds,
> It will be a display
> Of the sacred pledge
> Between myself and the earth."

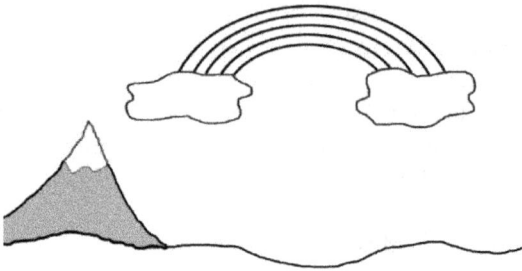

10

Living Beings

PRIOR TO THE FLOOD ACCOUNT, at the beginning of the Bible in Chapter One of Genesis, is the description of the Creation of the living beings of the world. Among those, it was written that these were created, in this order:

1) Birds - "fowl that may fly above the earth" (1:20)
2) Land Creatures – "bring forth the living creature after his kind, cattle, and creeping thing, and beast of the earth after his kind" (1:24)
3) And humans – "male and female created he them." (1:27 KJV)

Advancing chronologically to the flood account, in Genesis six, with the escalation of wrongdoing, there is the listing to "sweep aside" those same three categories in reverse order (humans, animals, birds):

6:7) "Gone
Will be the *humans*,

97

And further,
The animals,
From crawling beasts,
Up to *the birds* of the sky."

That reversed order (people, animals, birds) is repeatedly listed, at 6:18-20, 7:1-3, 7:13-14, 8:1, 8:18-19, and 9:2.

Placed among them were exceptions, using instead the original creation order (birds, animals, people) at 7:21 and 9:9, and people, birds, animals at 7:7-8. With the onset of the full force of the deluge, nearing the midpoint of the episode, the listing of 7:21 presents the original creation order as perishing:

7:21) And so perished …
Birds,
Livestock,
Animals of the wild,
The crawling serpents …
And with them,
Every person.

These duplicated inferences, for those of antiquity who may have been familiar also with the earlier Creation episode, would have added emphasis to the significance of the later Flood, as species were being dislodged and restored in awareness of the sequence in which they were originally formed. For an orator, skilled in the reciting of each of these major chronicles, that back and forth means of order within the Deluge event would have strengthened the presentation.

Moreover, the grammatical composition of the Flood episode further follows that of the Creation writing, as each focuses on a crucial individual (Adam, and then later Noah) and the family of each, surrounded with the living animals of the world. Also each family is provided with the divine decree to *be fruitful and multiply* or "grow greater in numbers" (in Genesis 1:28 for the first humans and in 8:17 for the descendants of Noah). Regarding the latter, the post-flood is a restructuring of the entire world, for by having undergone a cleansing and a rebirth, it is to be resettled and re-made.

In early Genesis, at 1:28, the abundant food supply was described: "I have given you every herb bearing seed" (KJV), and after the flood, this was expanded upon, and the eating of meat became allowable, at 9:3 with:

> 9:3) Each living creature
> Can now be food for you,
> As have been
> The fields of vegetables
> I had placed before
> All of you.

Just prior to the flood chronicle, there was a lengthy genealogical listing, all of Genesis chapter five, which consisted of 32 verses tracing the names and ages of those individuals from Adam all the way to Noah and his sons.

After the Deluge episode, all of Genesis ten, also 32 verses, is again an individual name listing, this time of Noah's sons' descendants. The two family trees, bookending the Flood coming between, are additional defining divisions.

As covered, Genesis six includes a listing of instructions given directly to Noah. There was the mandate consisting of directions on how to build an Ark, then briefly a statement of the Agreement with Noah, and then there followed additional commands regarding animal care.

That latter series of commands specified those to enter the Ark: Noah, his family, and then the animals which were listed by category. Also there were the directives to maintain those animals while upon the Ark. The long segment concludes with the statement that Noah had followed and accomplished all this. Those five chapter ending verses, with each of the responsibilities stressed, are:

> 6:18) *"You will be permitted*
> *To stay inside that Ark,*
> You and your sons,
> And your wife,
> And the wives of your sons
> With you.
> 19) *And including:*
> From among
> All the beasts of burden ...
> *You are to guide them*
> Into that Ark.
> Where *you are*
> *To provide for them* ...
> 20) For *you to take in* ...
> 21) And *you are to gather*
> All types of food to eat.
> *Collect it together"* ...
> 22) And *Noah carried through*
> On every part of this.
> What the *Lord God*
> *Had commanded of him,*
> *He did accomplish.*

After this lengthy listing, the very next words in the following chapter are five additional verses, again as commands, which come after Noah had completed his task of building the Ark.

Essentially a repeat, these verses are again a quoted first-person restatement of that which came immediately before. Beginning Genesis Chapter 7, they also function as a reminder, they begin the 'next Act' of the narrative, with the only addition being the distinction for clean (ritually pure) animals:

> 7:1) "*You are to enter!*
> *You*
> *And your entire family,*
> *Into the Ark ...*
> 2) Now – To the clean livestock,
> Those,
> Which are pure for ritual,
> Those,
> *You shall lead in ...*
> 5) And again,
> All that the *Lord God*
> *Commanded of him,*
> *Noah accomplished.*

What soon follows is the paired confirmation of Noah's full compliance with those twice-stated commands. But this time it was not in God's words spoken in the first person, but now as the third-person narrator's statements, to support the same information from this other perspective, indicating that the prior commands had been followed:

> 7:7) Noah
> With his sons,
> And his wife,
> And his sons' wives,
> *Made their way*
> *To within the Ark ...*
> 8) Also,
> From among
> The clean birds ...
> 9) *They went into the Ark*
> In toward Noah ...
> *In accordance with*
> *The directives*
> Of God.

And then yet again four verses later, with those getting into the Ark, there is the third-person restatement and declaration of that very same compliance:

> 7:13) *Having entered*
> *Into the Ark* were:
> Noah ...
> 15) *They came,*
> *Conducted by Noah,*
> *Into the Ark* ...
> 16) Those *entering* ...
> *They embarked*
> In the same manner
> As *God*
> *Had directed*
> To Noah.

The two initial sections contain first-person commands from God, that is, the one ending Chapter six and the one beginning Chapter seven, each on those to enter the vessel, with the second functioning as a new-Act reminder.

Those sections were followed shortly after by the two lengthy third-person confirmations of that compliance. As ancient recitation, this style of pairing clearly conforms to oration, either individually or accompanied by choral background, as echoing refrains.

In that latter third-person phrasing, one small section of wording at 7:7 has been phrased here as: "Made their way to within the Ark, to hold out *against the waters* of the forthcoming flood." This conforms to a crisis-confronting reading of that immediate action. It has usually been termed to *escape,* or *because of,* the waters of the flood.

The original words were, in Hebrew: *panim mayim,* or *facing waters,* but *panim* carried more of its additional and still literal meaning of *defiance,* to face in opposition, as confronting in a battle. In Greek, the phrase was: *dia tó hudor*, or *because of*, or the *fault of the water*. Making preparations to "hold out against" floodwaters is more attuned in current phrasing with a tenacious, continuing course of action, even to this day, of care-providers in combating the encroaching elements in flood regions.

Other smaller word assortments repeat within these segments. One short prepositional phrase, literally *from all*, in Greek *apo pas*, was used five times earlier in verse 6:19. The word *pas*, or *all* (also *each* or *every*), as previously mentioned, shows up with great frequency throughout the entire narrative. In that verse:

> 6:19) "From among
> *All* the beasts of burden,
> *All* the crawling serpents,
> *All* untamed of the wild,
> From *all* those that exist,
> Two by two,
> From *each* of these"

The latter part of that section of the verse uses the Greek duo, meaning two or a pair, and the word is repeated, balanced with *apo pas*, or: *duo duo apo pas*, translated as "Two by two from each."

A chapter later, as one of the repeats, verse 7:14 is very close in its phrasing:

> 7:14) *Every* untamed beast
> By their species,
> *All* livestock
> By their sort,
> Crawling creatures
> By their categories,
> Winged birds
> From their flocks

To mention the animals by their unique categories, in Greek it was *katá genos*. *Katá* is a preposition meaning *down from*, by way of, or according to, and *genos* is the noun meaning offspring, kindred, or family. The words *gene, genetics*, and *genealogy* stem from that root. With the word combination *katá genos* appearing in that verse, many English translations have usually repeated that as: According to, or after, their *kind*.

In Hebrew for the same terms, two forms of the word *min* (*meen*), also meaning kind or species, were used, with the expression *lə-mî-nâh* (according to their kind) used twice, followed by *lə-mî-nê-hû* (after its kind) used twice. As English has similarly explicit words to now express animal varieties, that phrasing, of species, sort, categories, and flocks, was applied in order to project the broad collection of classifications inferred, and also to replicate the chant-like resonance of the original.

Further along, in the latter section of the next Genesis chapter, chapter eight, there is again the listed order of humans and animals, this time with instructions to exit the Ark. There, once the Ark is back on dry land, those four-times intoned earlier instructions are recast in the opposite, in the form of the command for all to depart. The three verses 16 through 19 are an imbedded matching chiasm (shown here on the next page in form abc-x-cba) which maintains the priority of humans first, then the animals. As in the earlier format, Noah is first told directly by God, speaking in the first person, that Noah and his family, along with the other beings, are to exit the vessel so that, and this was placed at the midpoint of this phrasing, the repopulating of the earth can occur.

They do depart, and the repeating section of this mirrored segment follows, but in this latter portion, it is voiced now in the third person, with the narrator reaffirming the successful compliance, just as before. In that ancient format, here are the verses 8:16-19:

a)   *"Proceed forth, out from the Ark:*
b)   You, your wife, your sons,
        Your sons' wives with you!
        And all the living:
        The birds, the livestock,
        The wild animals of the ground,
c)   Lead them out as well.

x)   Then,
          Grow greater in numbers,
          Spread throughout the earth!"*

c)   And emerged:
b)   Noah and his wife, and his sons,
        And the wives of his sons with him.
        And every wild beast,
        The livestock, the winged birds,
        The crawling creatures,
        According to their type,
a)   *All departed the Ark.*

11

Firmament and Flood

IN THE BIBLICAL DESCRIPTION of the creation of the world within the very first chapter of Genesis, the term for a surrounding *firmament* was utilized directly: "Let there be a firmament in the midst of the waters, and let it divide the waters from the waters" (Genesis 1:6, KJV). Later, in the chapters of the description of the Deluge, that same signification of what was a solid firmament was expressed, indirectly, through the portrait of how all-inclusive waters, from the far side of the firmament, were released back upon the earth.

Examining that long-ago envisioning of the entire world within the cosmos will help illuminate the ancient interpretation of *firmament* (now at times also called a canopy or an expanse) and with it to more substantially explain the portrayal of the Great Flood, as it was understood by listeners of antiquity.

It was then an era in which learned individuals of that part of the world perceived the lands, the sea, and the sky, in their vision of the universe, their cosmology, as being contained below and within a type of great celestial arc, the Firmament, which was surrounded by additional waters.

The word *firmament* in Hebrew, *raqia*, was defined as an extended surface or a solid circular expanse. In Greek the term was *stereóma*, again a solid stationary body, a dome, an immovable support of steadfast durability.

Through the words of chroniclers, the Sun, the sky, the air, the moon and clouds, and the lands and seas, all were envisaged as being within that protective confine, that distant barrier. Vast oceans were conceived of as being contained on the far sides, having been split, separated by the Firmament, and beyond the perimeters of that celestial arc.

From that perspective, one such ocean was located far below the earth's solid ground, as unseen waters beneath the earth, and called the Great Deep Below or the Abyss. The other, upper portion of hidden ocean, that above the skies, was called the Waters Above.

The earth's visible seas and dry land were thereupon represented in writings as those which were placed essentially in the middle, between the sections of the Firmament. Also, the Heaven of Heavens above was perceived as even further beyond the sky, beyond the bulwark of the upper Firmament, and beyond even the Waters Above.

The concept is displayed on the next page:

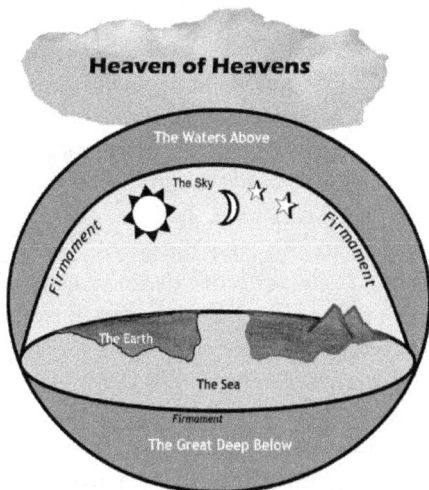

Concept of the Firmament

It was maintained in their thought that if the firmament barrier were at various entry points to have been unlocked, or to burst or to be broken, then those unseen waters, as violent far reaching outbreaks from beneath the ground and as torrents coming down from above the sky, would each come to engulf and cover the vulnerable land areas, meeting at the surface with disastrous and dramatic consequences.

The Deluge, the Great Flood, was therefore being described as caused by the intentional breaking of the containment barriers for the waters below, and of the opening of portals located throughout the upper Firmament, from which also the higher situated waters were unleashed. The result was that the world was then again entirely covered as one huge ocean, with no dry land, just as it was described earlier in Genesis, in its pre-land formation status, as during the original Creation.

In Genesis 6:17, after the instructions for building the

Ark, arriving floodwaters are acknowledged for the first time: "I will be inflicting a *flood* of water onto the earth." Translated as *flood*, the word in Hebrew was *mabbul* (*mab-bool'*). In Greek, the word was *kataklusmos*, referring to a deluge or flood from which the word cataclysm derives. The Hebrew term *mabbul* is written also later at various points in the Old Testament, but each time it is applied only in reference to this, the Flood of Noah, and to no other flood. *Mabbul* in scripture denoted not a frequent or seasonal type of flooding, but instead referred specifically to this one overwhelming deluge, this catastrophically destructive release of waters surging both upward from far beneath and down from on high, completely unique to this one episode. The wording emphasized the greater extent and all-inclusive nature of this one particular event, one contrasting entirely with what would be understood as conventional rainfall.

To designate the difference, other types of flooding in the Bible were characterized by separate Hebrew words, for example, in Daniel 9:26 (KJV), a prophecy concerning a city's destruction: "and the end thereof shall be with a flood." Instead of *mabbul*, the word *sheteph* was used there, meaning a flood or overflowing, but indicating a more localized type of calamity.

Returning to the Deluge, verse 7:4 again tells of the soon-to-be upcoming flooding. There, in parallel phrasing, it does so in Hebrew first with the verb *matar* (to pour down) and then repeats with *machah* (erase). In Greek there was first *epagó* (deliver) and then *exaleiphó* (cancel). The verb *exaleiphó* (from *ek*, out from, and *aleipho*, which initially in that language meant to wipe away) came later to mean to whitewash, and broadened further in meaning to cancel, as rubbing out an impression, or to cancel an obligation or entitlement. The verse, with the two paired segments shown separated, here is:

7:4) "I will deliver
A devastation
Of water to the world,
Forty days and forty nights.

I will wash away
Every entity I have made
From the entire surface
Of the earth."

The two phrases in this verse largely reinforce one another, with the second being a logical result of the first.

Applying that wording to the living of the world emphasized the impending totality of the *cancellation* process through flooding. Given the strong connection between the verse's two phrases, by using first the *delivering of water*, and then continuing the concept with *wash away*, they more closely approach their original pairing.

Moving forward, in Genesis 7:11 it states in original language that the Great Flood began with waters rushing forth, out from the lower abyss and simultaneously pouring downward, as with waterfalls, from the sky. What are called "*bulging reservoirs* buried deep below" and "*towering enclosures* holding oceans above the skies" were opened, with each expelling vast amounts of water from below and from above, onto the earth.

From the buried reservoirs, the text described the deeply suppressed waters as breaking loose and spewing onto the world's surface from beneath. The matching paired words, "towering enclosures" were expressed as rapidly opening downward to release waters originating from above the sky. That downward action possessed features with recognizable similarity of purpose to commonplace water regulation fixtures of that era, as with land-based gates or sluices, which could be opened to release their contents.

With characteristics identifiable in ancient times as those which could regulate varying volumes of flow, both the moving-upward accumulation and the downward gushing would be seen as operating in a conceptually related manner to how water might rapidly emerge from within broken or overflowing wells, or could be expelled from engorged irrigation channels, or even as thick smoke from quick-burning material would heavily issue through a vented chimney. The purposes of man-made wells, channels, and chimneys, that is, to function as controlled conduits which governed the release of fluctuating amounts, was routine to people of the time. By using those ordinary everyday concepts, and by then expounding upon them with reciprocal descriptions of what was spilling forth from both the contents of the vast seas far below and from the oceans beyond the sky, listeners of then could visualize how the extensive waters would meet, to cover the Earth's surface.

At 7:11 the onrush of the tumultuous outbreak is mirrored in phrasing, as in the original scripture:

a)   Burst apart
b)   All the bulging reservoirs
           Buried deep below
b)   And the towering enclosures
           Holding oceans above the skies
a)   Flung open.

To begin and end the phrase were two complementary action verbs, each of which referred to an expulsion, a means of release through a type of fissure. The first of which ("burst apart") introduced the barrage of water from below. In Hebrew, the verb was *baqa*, also translated as split open or burst apart. Greek used *rhégnumi*, or, written: εϱϱάγησαν, meaning to burst, to tear forth, to break asunder.

To mirror that, a final accompanying verb form ("flung

open") for the torrential onslaught from the sky completed the matched expression. The action verb in Hebrew was *pathach* (*paw-thakh´*) and meaning to set free, to loosen, or to be flung open. In Greek that verb was *anoigó*, or as actually written in third person plural, ηνεώχθησαν, meaning *they were opened*, or flung open.

For the first of the two middle expressions, "all the bulging reservoirs buried deep below," in Hebrew three terms were combined. First was *mayan*, the underground water containment, here called the "reservoirs," and was defined long ago as wells, springs, or fountains. Adjoining it were *tehom*, meaning deep, a sea of the abyss, and then *rab*, meaning abundance or great amount. Together they literally form *great deep wells*, or large areas of subterranean waters.

The same phrase in Greek consisted of *pégé*, and in the plural, water sources, or fountains, springs, wells of the *abussos*, meaning the abyss, the boundless depth, or together, wells of the abyss. Later in the Bible, the terms *mayan* (Hebrew) or *pégé* (Greek) are frequent. Their next usage after the flood episode is at Leviticus 11:36: "A fountain or pit, wherein there is plenty of water" (KJV), and in each successive usage, directly or metaphorically, the reference is to an area collecting or containing typically abundant depths of water.

For the next, the second of the two middle expressions: "And the towering enclosures holding oceans above the skies," implied looking upward, describing the concept of bulwarks holding back waters from far on high. For the expression, in Hebrew first came the word *arubbah*, that is, lattices or sluices. They were types of gate or hatch fixtures which can be opened and closed. It was paired with *shamayim*, meaning of the visible heaven, the sky. Those enclosures, water conduits, have been subsequently termed *windows*, or *floodgates*. The word *arubbah* appears nine times in the Old Testament scripture, and each time it can be viewed as a type of portal, one that ends with, or has within, a lattice-like feature, designed for opening, and the word was often used to describe a dramatic outpouring. For example, in Isaiah 24:18: "For the windows from on high are open, and the foundations of the earth do shake." In Hosea 13:3 the same word, for a different item now but used then for a similar conceptual sense, was called chimney, with: "and as the smoke out of the chimney" (both KJV).

In Greek the same up-above referencing terms were first: *katarithmeó*, with one meaning being *cataracts* or contained torrents or waterfalls. However, another and related meaning of the word was as a dungeon or a vault, an area of confinement. The word was placed with *ouranos*, the sky, the visible heavens, or heights beyond, and then came the ending *anoigó*, again meaning to be set free or flung open.

As with a rapid letting loose from a restraint, one can apprehend the flinging open and pouring of waters down from above, being released to fall to the earth's surface.

The beginning words, in either language, those of *bursting apart* from the reservoirs below, did not use the same term as that ending term, the down from above type of pouring. Instead, for the waters from below, it implied a breach or fracturing. Picturing today, for example, a large underground storage tank, one which might experience a rupture or fissure, the immediate effect would not necessarily involve a geyser-like upward eruption, but instead it is much more likely there would be extensive ground saturation, quickly and potentially becoming flood-like.

What those of long ago were hearing would have elicited such impressions, as many could have been aware of the potential aggregate havoc from water-well breakages, and conversely of downward rapid freeing of higher constricted waters. A land saturation would accordingly be in contrast with a waterfall-like surge from an ocean far above, but each action, whether from below or from above, would have been seen in vivid terms as accomplishing a shared outcome, that of unprecedented long-term flooding.

Again, no knowledge of written Greek script is required to observe this brief but expressive long-ago phrasing, and as before, by simply noting the appearance of these words, especially their suffixes ending each of the four lines in Greek (accompanied by literal English), the recognizable lyrical and paralleling aspects of the wording may become more evident. The mirroring, pervasive throughout the narrative, can be better appreciated by actually 'seeing' it here. Again, from 7:11:

a) ερράγησαν
    burst-forth-they
b)   πάσαι αι πηγαί της αβύσσου
        all   the wells of abyss
b)   και οι καταρράκται τον ονρανού
        and the cataracts of   sky
a)   ηνεώχθησαν
        flung-open-they

Centuries later, with the Vulgate translation of the Bible, this verse in Latin also maintained that early word configuration, as it began and ended with verbs in the same manner. Here is 7:11, in Latin and English:

rupti sunt	Broken were
omnes fonts	all fountains
abyssi magnae	abyss great
et	and
cataractae caeli	cataracts sky
apertae sunt	Opened were

In the next chapter, 8, to bring an end to the long continuance of the outpouring, similar reciprocal phrasing recounted the complete reversal of the actions, the restoration, the shutting back of those lower and upper enclosures, at 8:2:

> And were set firm:
>> Both the reservoirs
>> From the deep below,
>> And the enclosures
>> Above the sky.
>> The inundation
>> From the heavens
> Was held back.

The two starting and ending verb forms here: *set firm* and *held back*, each describe what would hold in check any further outpour, for the repair or shutting of those same bottom and top features would stop the imposition of additional waters.

There is some variation between Hebrew and Greek wording for this, to express those actions of closing. In Hebrew, the two verbs were first *caker (saw-kar´)* meaning to *stop up*, or to tightly shut, to firmly restrict, or in other circumstances, to surrender over or to silence. Then late in the verse is the associated verb *kala*, meaning to shut or to restrain, to hold back.

In Greek, there was a slightly different approach, as first the lower and upper breakages or mechanisms, earlier not visible, were said here to now be *revealed*, and the verse ends with the fixtures from above now being *restrained*. The verse begins with *apokaluptó*, meaning to uncover. The word apocalypse, a revelation or revealing concerning a cataclysm, derives from this word. The latter verb, *sunechó (soon-ekh´-o)*, meant *pressing together*, compressing, hemming in, or to *hold fast*. In a somewhat associated, and much later nautical attribute, *to batten down the hatches* means to prevent water from entering, and possesses a similar meaning to that type of restraining.

Proceeding to earlier English translations, in the Bible

of the theologian John Wycliffe (1395), and returning back to that portion of verse 7:11, at the first usage of the term for the lower waters, those of the Abyss, there the word *wells* was selected, and for the upper skyward heavenly fixtures the word *windows* was chosen. In updated spelling, it was:

> All the wells of the great sea were broken, and the windows of heaven were opened.

In what became established in English, the Tyndale (1534), Geneva (1560) and King James (1611) phrasings in that verse were identical:

> Were all the fountains of the great deep broken up, and the windows of heaven were opened.

As those of today are mostly unacquainted with that ancient visualization of the world, a world then thought of as located within unseen oceans both below and above, and to be hearing now of *wells* or *fountains* or *windows*, such contemporary terms no longer capture the impression of extensiveness of volume which was then being described.

Presently, few would ever encounter a working well, much less conceive of the damage or potentially life-threatening consequences of one broken. What's more, fountains now are usually thought of as decorative, as safely controlled sprays stationed for expensive ostentation in front of high-end buildings or within landscaped parks. Also, and continuing with modern alterations of word meanings, windows have the image now of transparent glass, which was not at all what they of the time recognized, and contemporary glass windows in many larger structures are not designed to even be opened, thereby missing the basis entirely for unleashed waters.

To once again express the degree of a destructive inundation, delivered in enormous aggregation from otherwise deep or far-away locations, now more pointedly aligned voicing is needed to better describe what then was being depicted as having taken place, as an orator's words would have potentially astounded a long-ago group of listeners.

Corresponding in degree to distant times, as a rule individuals now are aware of what modern reservoirs are, and the large amounts of water they may possess. Individuals today also can likely envision an abstraction of containment-type enclosures located high above, and how they might function if to impound unseen waters. In the narrative of the Flood, where even the word for a firmament is not directly mentioned, to more properly accord the mental imagery of massive water releases, the terms "reservoirs" and "enclosures," to contain what were viewed as essentially "oceans," can better reflect those original representations.

Within the narrative, the common term *windows* has often historically been applied in English to describe three otherwise separate words relating to two different upper segments of the Ark, and then to the openings within the upper Firmament. The singular *window* had in some early translations in 6:16 referred to the narrowed connecting point at the top of the Ark. For that, both the Geneva Bible and King James Version stated: "a window shalt thou make to the ark."

Secondly, proceeding to the upper firmament openings in chapters 7 and 8, earlier translations, as cited, employed *windows of heaven* for what here are termed "towering enclosures" which were "above the skies."

Third, also in Genesis 8, at verse 8:6, the word *window* additionally has been assigned for the small window of the Ark that Noah opened to first release the raven and then the dove.

However, both in Hebrew (*tsohar, arubbah*, and *challon*) and in Greek (*episunagó, katarithmeó*, and *thuris*) separate words were exercised for each of those three terms. To reinstate the more scriptural usages, this translation returns to the three separate designations, not embracing window for the first two instances, but instead for those: In the first instance, "Connect it from above," then in the second, in the sky, "enclosures." For the third, "window" is used only at 8:6 with: "Noah opened the small window of the Ark." Later in this book, chapter 13 (The Drying of Land) explains the small window item in greater detail.

12

The Flood's Duration
and the Turning Point

THE FLOOD'S DURATION over several months is emphasized throughout the narrative by the mirrored attributions to the increasing and then declining numbers of days to describe it. At the start of Genesis seven is the command to enter the Ark, and then with the land's re-emergence in chapter 8 is the command to depart:

> 7:1) And then the Lord God
> Said to Noah:
> "You are to enter!
> You,
> And your entire family,
> Into the Ark."

> 8:15) Then the Lord God
> Spoke to Noah, saying:
> 16) "Proceed forth,
> Out from the Ark:

You,
Your wife,
Your sons,
Your sons' wives with you!"

Between that one and a half chapter span from 7:1 to 8:15 is the depiction of the full Flood, and throughout that section, the Flood's continuance, as it progressed, is repeatedly stressed. Its rising and falling phases are described as proportionately incrementing and then decreasing in numbered days as they surround the episodic midpoint, the verse at 8:1.

First, to acknowledge the multiple references of when the Flood begins, the alternating numbers, easily memorable when being heard, reflect a fixed increasing pattern as Genesis seven proceeds:
7,40,40 - 7,40,40 - 40,40,150.

7:4) It is to be,
In *seven days*,
I will deliver
A devastation of water
To the world,
Forty days and forty nights.

7:10) And so,
After seven days,
The tumultuous flood
Was set in force

7:12) Waters were released
Onto the earth,
Forty days and forty nights.

7:17) The flooding kept on
Those *forty days and forty nights*

7:24) And the waters
Stood at those heights
Upon the earth
One hundred and fifty days.

After the numbers advance in chapter seven, there is the centrally placed pivot point at 8:1, which tells of God being mindful of those on the Ark and then acting to curtail the flooding. After that, with the waters slowly abating, the numbers of intervening days, as with the water levels, begin to recede and decline, back from 150 to 40 to 7 days, through the early part of chapter eight. The entire chronology is:

In 7 days the flood will begin
For 40 days and 40 nights *(7:4)*
After 7 days, flood upon the world *(7:10)*
40 days and 40 nights, gushing waters *(7:12)*
40 days and 40 nights of flood *(7:17)*
Covering waters to last 150 days *(7:24)*
The Lord, mindful of Noah
Brought forth a breath of wind *(8:1)*
After the 150 days, waters recede *(8:3)*
40 days later, Noah opened window *(8:6)*
Sent forth raven and dove, dove returned *(8:9)*
7 days waiting, sent dove again *(8:10)*
Dove returned with olive leaf *(8:11)*
7 more days waiting, sent dove again,
It did not return *(8:12)*

At the midpoint, verse 8:1, the account states that the thoughts of God turned back to those on the Ark, and God then brought about a halt to the further increase of flooding. This represents the pivotal element, the 'X' hub, the verse at the epicenter of not only the number sequence but of the entire narrative. This is the juncture at which God intervenes and suppresses the rising of the waters by means of a calming breath of wind, and it is this threshold from which the renewal actions then take place. From this point, the previous events are now mirrored episodically in reverse, which the declining numbers serve to affirm.

Just prior to this juncture, at the very end of chapter seven, the four verses 7:21-24 summarize the events leading up to that, and are also a cue to what, later in inverse order, would be upcoming.

The first two of those four verses, 21 and 22, are themselves in mirrored form, the first beginning with "perished" (and then the Creation order of birds, animals, people) and the second verse ending with "passed away."

> 7:21) And *so perished*
> All the living
> Which had before
> Been active
> Across the vast regions:
> Birds,
> Livestock,
> Animals of the wild,
> Crawling serpents,
> All which moved
> Over the surface,
> And with them,
> Every person.
> 22) They that had breathed
> With spirit of life,
> They, anywhere
> Upon the lands,
> All *passed away.*

In both Hebrew and Greek, each was not only mirrored with the start and finishing verbs, but within them both, there were repeating variations for words of activity or living movement ("been *active*" then "*moved* over the surface" and "*breathed* with spirit of life") which contrast with the surrounding terms for their repose ("perished" and "passed away"), the ending of their lives. The next verse, 7:23, adds to this closing emphasis, reasserting it, this time with the Creation order reversed (people, animals, birds):

> 7:23) Taken from existence
> Was their every trace
> Off the face of the earth:
> From humans,
> Animals,
> Crawling serpents,
> And birds of the sky,
> None any longer
> Were alive in the world.

The final verse, 7:24, coming after the prior numbered instances of sevens and forties, finishes with the first reference (of only two) to the longer duration of one hundred and fifty days.

> 24) And the waters
> Stood at those heights
> Upon the earth
> One hundred and fifty days.

These chapter-ending verses sum up the critical series of events to have come about thus far, and they decidedly conclude the episode's first half. As oration, they observe the ancient harmonization of first, a powerful statement, immediately resoundingly echoed by an equally powerful restatement.

If a speaker's long pause were to have been situated here, at the completion of the chapter, it would have functioned not only as a forceful cessation of all previous events, but by stopping after having set forth the prolonged 150 day duration, it would add prominence, advancing the impact. As part of an episodic build-up, it would effectively have left listeners at a suspenseful peak, to await the next upcoming actions.

Thus, with a presenter's rest or audience break here, after the two opening chapters of the episode, and ending the first half of the narrative, it formulated an ideal dramatic interlude, one that can be directly perceived as a 'second act' culmination, and the spot at which to place an appropriate 'intermission.' This summary compendium would have left first time and even veteran listeners in anticipation of what was to come.

What did come, the first verse of chapter eight, serves as a resumption after the practicable intermission. The verse introduces the second half of the total episode, of two more biblical chapters, and it stands as the central axis, the 'X' point, with the calming and decisive intervention by God. Here is that 'reopening' verse:

> 8:1) And it was, that God
> Came to bring back to mind:
> > Noah,
> > All the untamed beasts,
> > All the livestock,
> > All the winged birds,
> > All the crawling serpents,
> > The many, there with him,
> > Inside the Ark.
> And it was then, that God
> Proceeded to bring forth:
> > A transcendent
> > Breath of wind
> > Across the world,
> > Which calmed the water.

The verse at its most basic contains within it a recap, a restatement of the immediately preceding verses 7:23-24.

For those 'late-seating,' or all, returning audience members, it begins by reaffirming what had earlier occurred, and on a more moderating note. First, its opening clause, "God came to bring back to mind Noah" serves as a reminder, as an orator would be reminding the listeners what had just transpired before a break.

Continuing, to the midsection of the verse, those within the Ark ("The many") listed after Noah, were yet again specified, another expressive reminder. A variation in wording between the two ancient languages occurs here, regarding the animal categories. In Hebrew the text designates two groupings, first *chay* (wild animals, untamed beasts), followed by *behemah* (domesticated animals). In Greek there are four: *Thérion* (wild animals), *kténos* (domesticated animals), *peteinon* (birds), and *herpeton* (creeping creatures, reptiles), fully repeating the four which were listed earlier, those as perishing in 7:21, and prior to the break. In each language here at 8:1 they were placed after Noah's name and before the wording of "there with him inside the Ark."

Coming after this listing, introduced in 8:1 is a new, yet again vividly impressive and matching element for an audience. In this third segment, it goes on to state that God, as with the much earlier initiating of the flood, again markedly intervened, but this time "proceeded to bring forth a transcendent breath of wind" to render tranquil the surface. This is the turning-point juncture in the narrative, the act which sets in motion the entire sequence of reversing events.

This returning wording bears close examination; first, because the verse was written even within itself in a paralleled fashion, with the symmetry characteristic of the entire episode. Its introductory words, those of God's recalling thoughts, have a primary purpose of linking with and enhancing the significance of the verse's closing phrasing, that of God's definitive yet calming action. Between those segments is the reminder listing of the survivors, those which were sheltered within the Ark.

In this single verse, the sections serve as a major transformative development. While they contain many of the narrative's most vital elements, in translation their paired beginning and ending passages can be downplayed or not accorded significant weight if not appropriately given the original connecting phrasing and emphasis.

For example, as to how this verse has been worded in English, the 1395 Wycliffe Bible translation articulated the concept of God's focusing returned awareness in its first lines, using: 'the Lord had mind of Noah' (original spelling: 'the Lord hadde mynde of Noe') which made plain the internalization of thought. But many later versions by others instead have come to use the abbreviated choice of words that God *remembered* Noah and the others; and then late in the same verse would often use just the wording that God had *made* or *sent a wind* over the earth.

Those particular terms don't connote for readers now the full implication or substantive linking of those once much more involved interconnecting declarations.

In English today, *remembered* suggests that if someone remembers, they might also earlier have forgotten, and that term doesn't engage the totality of the awareness that was originally being described. Correspondingly, the prevalent later phrasing of *sent a wind* does not directly relate to any current meaning of *remembering*.

As once more stirringly clear ancient remarks, the actual scriptural terms for *remember* and *sent a wind* did more intrinsically connect as a beginning and ending, they were decidedly attuned to one another. In those languages, there was a definite pairing between the initial resuming of thought and the subsequent expressed action.

To better reflect that, the pairing is here phrased as first "That God came to bring back to mind" those on the Ark, and closes with the restorative "That God proceeded to bring forth a transcendent breath of wind," as they are, in combination, more reciprocally affiliated.

In Hebrew, the term used for the recollection was *zakar*, which means *to bring to mind*, to cognitively consider, and it also meant to *mark*, to take note of, to *record* or transcribe.

In Greek the term for the same first phrasing: "To bring back to mind" was the lengthier *anamimnéskó (an-am-im-nace´-ko)*, meaning in part to *remind* oneself, to call to mind. It also referred to *recording*, marking for posterity.

Later in the Bible, the same word (Hebrew *zakar*, Greek *anamimnéskô*) was used in 1 Kings 4:3: "Jehoshaphat the son of Ahilud, the recorder" (KJV), for one who was the writer of the records.

In like manner, the intricate verb *anamimnéskó*, written 'ανεμνήσθη,' meant not just a *record* or *recollection*, but here in 8:1 more than that, it suggested a *process* of recall, to retrace one's marked course of memory, to journey to where remembrance will lead. To state it more comprehensively as "came to bring back to mind" can better reflect that more involved path of unfolding retrospection.

Returning to Hebrew, and the third segment of the verse ("God proceeded to bring forth a transcendent breath of wind"), the wind phrasing begins with *abar*, meaning to *send through* or to *pass through*. Then comes the word *Elohim*, God, followed by *ruach (roo´-akh)*, defined as *wind* or *air* or *breath*, but also in addition it carried the higher connected meaning of *spirit* and as symbolic of *life*. Together, the literal terms are: *From God, the breath/spirit passed through*.

In Greek, to compliment the earlier *anamimnéskó* there is also, again late in 8:1, a near-identical word combination: *Epagó, Theos*, and *pneuma*. First comes the verb *epagó*, written 'επήγαγεν,' meaning *to bring forth*, or when used earlier at 6:17, *to inflict*, "I will be *inflicting* a flood of water onto the earth") and in 7:4, to *deliver* ("I will *deliver* a devastation of water.") In 8:1, after *epagó*, comes the term *Theos*, God, which was matched with the word *pneuma (nyoo´-mah)*, externally meaning *wind, breeze, air movement*, or *breath*, and internally *spirit*, and in this verse as a "breath of wind" which embodies the more understood meaning of the word of long ago. Breathing or air-related terms in English such as *pneumonia* or *pneumatic*, with their silent 'p' derive from that root.

Reinforcing the connection between the two mirrored phrases of 8:1, at its beginning, God's thoughts, and then later in the verse, God's action, observing each in literal Greek will assist in demonstrating their more obvious association, more apparent to those of the times, as they in script looked (and sounded) quite comparable to one another. They are:

και ανεμνήσθη ο θεός του Νώε
And reminded The God he Noah

και επήγαγεν ο θεός πνεύμα
And brought The God breath/wind

That final word *pneuma* (πνεύμα) above, appeared earlier in the episode, first within 6:17, where God stated: "All beings which take in their *breath* of life" and then at 7:15 with: "Beings which embody the *breath* of life." In Greek *pneuma*, as with the Hebrew word *ruach*, carried the meaning of not just *breath/wind*, but additionally the higher meaning of *spirit*, or, with *pneuma*, a *soul, holy Spirit*.

Looking to a point much earlier in the Bible, at the very beginning of Genesis, in describing the creation of the world, the same words, *ruach* or *pneuma*, have been traditionally translated there, at that point, rather than as *wind* on waters, but instead as *spirit*, where in the second verse of the Bible, 1:2: "And the Spirit of God moved upon the face of the waters" (KJV).

Later in the Bible, in the Book of Numbers, 11:31, the same two words, *ruach/pneuma*, were used as *wind*, with: "There went forth a wind from the LORD, and brought quails from the sea" (Geneva and KJV).

Still later in the Bible, in the Book of Job, 12:10, *ruach* and *pneuma* were then used as *breath* where both the Geneva Bible and the King James Version there state:

> In whose hand is the soul of every living thing, and the breath of all mankind.

With that varied phrasing in mind, with *spirit* and *wind* and *breath* in prior centuries in English being used for the same ancient words, and returning now to that appearance in verse 8:1, an otherwise less-than-clear association between when God *remembered* and then *sent a wind*, becomes a great deal more.

As mentioned earlier, in a time of antiquity when thinking, the thought process, was believed to originate from the heart, then breathing, also from the chest, was perceived as more closely related physically to thought, to their connection.

By now saying, as in the ancient languages, that God brought all of them "back to mind" and then resultantly brought to the waters a profound "transcendent breath of wind," exhaling the breath as of the body, that wording allows the verbal interconnectivity between first *thought* and then a physical/spiritual *act* of higher resolution, as perceived long ago, to become more mutually apparent.

While both the Hebrew *ruach* and Greek *pneuma* were each one emphatic and multifaceted word, that same more intricate concept today is no longer as well articulated with just one single word. Thus here at 8:1 "a transcendent breath of wind" is, in that same approach, better able to be viewed now, as then, as a *soul's breath* across the waters over the earth.

It can be clarified further by looking at two not entirely dissimilar words to the Greek *anamimnéskó* ("to bring back to mind.") In particular, there were two related later terms in Latin language, *animus* and *anima*, each with overlapping meanings of higher *soul* or *spirit*. The Latin *animus* additionally has a root meaning of *mind* and *intellect*, while *anima* has a root meaning of physical *breath* from the body, and also of *life force*. This indicated an interplay of the two words, *animus* and *anima*, that between mind and body, or that of higher spiritual thinking and that of internal breath-originated higher spiritual action. In Eastern thought, the oppositional yet complimentary aspects of *yin* and *yang*, for example rest and movement, also reflect that concept.

Viewing the Greek *anamimnéskó* as an intellectual observation by God, as in effect a scheduled 'checking in' on Noah, it leads in a path more directly to God's then issuing forth the more physical and spiritual aspects of *pneuma*, the soul's breath of wind, the outpouring as with one issuing a cure, as the beginning of the solution. Both steps, first the observational step, followed by the more evident step of bringing forth "a transcendent breath of wind" allow that dual combination to be better perceived, each as steps in a twofold process. As with God's earlier forming man and then breathing life therein, so it was by turning focus back toward those on the Ark and then physically issuing a manifestation of the breath of life to restore a stillness to their rising and falling enclosed world through an encompassing calming breath of air. That expression, that divine expulsion of breath, a release of the healing aspect of Soul, marked the beginning of the restorative events, the reversal of the turmoil which came before, and set forth the full recovery which was to come.

The significance of the impact of winds over waters has been a recurring theme throughout history, and the perception of salvation by means of a godly breath is acknowledged in other cultures as well. For example, the Japanese word *kamikaze*, in more recent times referring to specialized World War II pilots, is translated literally as *divine wind*. *Kami* is the word for god, spirit, or divinity, and *kaze* for wind. The word originally referred to a severe storm, specifically to the typhoon which spared the islands of Japan from invasion by destroying the naval fleets of Emperor Kublai Khan of China in the year 1281.

This verse 8:1, occupying the critical 'X' or the mirroring's central element, and initiating the second half of the entire narrative, is demonstrably the core, that which contains an essential intersecting message, that of restoration.

Put succinctly, it describes God's resuming an awareness of those alive, and then acting from within to save them, to realign a course for humanity and all of the air-breathing animal kingdom. That dispatching, that intervention, through its duality of original wording and affixed at the beginning of the second half of the episode, was being made emphatically clear to the listeners of that time. It changed the direction of the narrative, setting the tone for the less hectic, more rejuvenating remaining half.

Following this key midpoint verse of 8:1, the actions go further in continuing to undo the turmoil. After the waves were suppressed, there are reversing processes in mirrored form which extinguish the rising waters of the prior Genesis chapter. Continuing with the second and third verses of chapter 8:

> 8:2) Further inundation
> From the heavens
> Was held back.
> 3) It followed,
> That after
> One hundred and fifty days,
> The waters
> Coursing over the earth
> Then were drawing away.

The prior pronouncement which concluded chapter seven had specified that the waters covered the land for 150 days. Here, just three verses (and an intermission) later, that same number 150 is stated again.

Coming between is the listing of those within the Ark at

8:1, and as with that listing, this number 150 can be viewed as a reminder, a repeat. It alludes to the time after the waters were shut off, after the 'spigots' were closed at the end of the devastating first forty days. At that point, the earth blanketing waters did not immediately dissipate; the text states that they remained.

With the entire narrative viewed in echoing fashion, rather quickly returning to that 150 day length of the fully covering waters of the flood at 8:3 serves again to let it be known to an audience, as before the orator's break, that this was how long the high waters lasted, with no land to be seen, not even mountaintops.

Thus it can be interpreted that the only two mentions of the 150 days, the one at the end of chapter 7, and the one following early in chapter 8, each referred to the same circumstance, that in which there was no visible land, and the second, at 8:3, is a repetition, as with so many of the episode's phrasings. The text states that after this protracted period, the high waters began to lower, with a long slow decline of levels.

For clarification, to review the total chronology, the Flood begins earlier, in chapter 7:

> 7:11) It being
> The six hundredth year
> Of Noah's life,
> In its second month,
> On the twenty seventh
> Day of the month,
> On that day
> Burst apart
> All the bulging reservoirs

It states that the flood began (with more numerical precision, specifically the second month, and twenty seventh day) and then 40 days (and nights) pass, and God then became mindful and brought forth the breath of wind (at 8:1). The openings for the waters of above and below are closed (at 8:2) and the further rising of waters is discontinued. Then later, a time of slowly declining residual flood water begins. The long term receding is confirmed, continuing at 8:3:

> 8:3) Their levels
> Dropped lower.
> 4) In the seventh month,
> On the twenty seventh day,
> The Ark
> Came to a halt
> Above the mountains
> Of Ararat.

In 8:3, after the 150 days are stated the second time, what immediately follows in 8:4 is a mention of a later specific month and day (the *seventh* month, twenty *seventh* day). With the earlier statement (at 7:11) of the 2nd month, 27th day, then this 7th month, 27th day, and thirty-day months meant that five months had passed, 150 days, confirming the total, affirming the count for those ancient listeners.

A numerical text difference occurs here, as, in Greek, in verses 7:11, 8:4, and 8:14, the day of the 27th is listed each time. However, in Hebrew, in verse 7:11 and 8:4, the day of the 17th is listed, and only in 8:14 is it the 27th.

While many explanations have been proposed (including the easy one, scribal error), a more likely scenario is that there were regional, leading to textual, variations in the long-term usages of lunar calendars (with an average of shorter 27 to 30 day months and 354 day years) in antiquity.

There is a comparative circumstance in more modern times, specifically the near-worldwide adoption of the Gregorian calendar from the earlier Julian calendar, which had been in use since the Roman era. The two calendars over time had developed an approximate ten-day variation, and the gradual conversion from the older to the newer took centuries, nation by nation, over the years from 1582 to 1926.

Returning to the flood chronology in days, while there was non-uniformity in the lengths of some months, nonetheless, both the Hebrew and Greek versions were each internally consistent.

The text stresses that well after the specified day of start of the flood, and even after the Ark had ceased movement, there still was nothing but water visible. While the Ark's hull below the surface settled, and with the Ark situated at a high elevation, it implied to listeners that no land features whatsoever were yet to be seen, even if one within were to look directly out or below.

The narrative mentioned in the next verse that, later on, the highest features began to emerge, and numbers relating to duration continued:

8:5) With lapping waters
In gradual decline,
And when the passing days
Reached the first
Of the tenth month,
The peaks of the mountains
Had reappeared.

8:6) There,
After forty days had passed,
Noah opened the small window

8:13) And it came to be,
Noah reached in his life
The age of six hundred and one.
In that same month,
On the first day of the month,

The water had receded
From more of the world.

8:14) In the next, the second month,
On the twenty seventh
Day of the month,
The land's surface
Had become fully dry.
15) Then the Lord God
Spoke to Noah, saying:
16) "Proceed forth"

With land described as slowly re-emerging amongst lowland pockets of flooding, and months passing, the Flood as narrated had taken approximately a year, from beginning to end, before the land had fully dried. While a flood's after effects can be long term, a typical flood, rising and falling, usually lasts a few hours, or rarely more than a few days. Of the narrative of the Deluge, it described a duration of significant momentousness to listeners.

Relating to the beginning, middle, and ending aspects of the entire narrative, the connection with and similarity in syntax to the episode's opening verses, specifically 6:6 and 6:7, with the center verse of 8:1, and then later, with the departure from the Ark and aftermath at 8:21, all of this helps further demonstrate the unity and affiliation of actions, and of verse structure.

The early verses, those of 6:6-7, again are:

6:6) God reflected:
On having created
People upon the earth.
After profound deliberation,
7) God spoke:
"I am about
To sweep aside

> Humanity,
> Those I have formed,
> Any to be seen on earth.
> Gone
> Will be the humans,
> And further,
> The animals."

In Greek, 6:6 began with the lengthy verb *enthumeomai* ("reflected") in which God gave thought to the wrongful actions of humanity. Similarly in style, verse 8:1 began with the related opening verb of *anamimnéskó* ("to bring back to mind.")

After these beginnings, at verse 6:7 there is a listing of first people and then animals, while verse 8:1 also contains an equivalent listing, of those people and animals within the Ark.

Back at verse 6:7, it states God's decision "to sweep aside" most on earth, as 8:1 reverses that, and concludes with God's earth-altering "breath of wind" to calm the waters.

Still later, at the closing of the same chapter 8, after the occupants' departure from the Ark, the text returns, at 8:21, to a development also closely matching the opening wording in 6:5-7.

That verse in full came immediately after Noah had built an altar and had sacrificed burnt offerings.

Again, this sizable verse encapsulates God's response to that act of devotion, and is the next-to-last verse of the chapter:

> 8:21) And thus
> The Lord God decided:
> "In giving thought,
> I will not
> Compound the condemnation
> Of the lands of the earth,

Despite the dealings
Of humanity.
And while the notions
Of human beings
Still incline toward
The wrongdoing of youth,
I will not again
Strike down
All the living
In such manner
As I have done."

Early here in 8:21, to indicate God's inner thought, it is expressed as "decided" or to inwardly speak, and in the next line comes "giving thought" as God here is not speaking directly to Noah. In Greek wording, the term for "decided" was expressed with *epo*, to say, to decide, or to intend. It was followed in the next wording by the multi-used term *dianeuó*, in *giving thought*. Then later in the Greek phrasing, alliteratively continued the terms *dia*, meaning *despite* or *on account of*, and *dianoia*, meaning *of mind*, or less formally, *notions*, again contrasting imperfect human nature with God's higher level of thought. (The ancient 'd' sound alliteration has been preserved here with: "Despite the dealings.")

So it relates at 8:21 that God, as in the two previous instances (the narrative's beginning and midsection), gives mind to, and then takes resolute action, and in the latter case, it is to promise to spare the earth this type of future devastation.

To further bolster the connectedness within these verse segments is the inclusive presence of several significant keywords. In the opening verse, 6:5, in the central 8:1, and in 8:21, the word for *every* or *all* (Hebrew *kol*, Greek *pas*) was employed. It was used twice in 6:5: "Every individual" and "all over the world." In Greek, the word *pas* was used four times in 8:1 alone to refer to the animal types: "*All* the untamed beasts" and those that followed. "All the living" occurs in 8:21. Additionally, the Hebrew term *erets* or the Greek *gé*, the *world*, the *earth*, appears in each of these strategic verses, underscoring priority within the chronicle.

This particular latter verse, 8:21, was confirming that after *all* that had ensued, here now was the beginning of a final resolution. In translation it is difficult, as mentioned, to capture 'tone' or a shift in wording, to convey a not quite expressed undercurrent of meaning, which is more easily understood in speech. What comes through in the original is a tone, somewhat as with a parent assessing a willful but nonetheless devoted child. Written in the first person, it suggests a caregiving reaction, paraphrased, of: *I am aware they make mistakes, but despite that, I understand and accept them.*

In this verse a negative "I will not" is repeated ("*I will not* compound" and "*I will not* again strike down"), both giving emphasis to the assurance that, despite humanity's flaws, despite their continued focus upon the wrongful and excessive thoughts of youth, here now was the pledge to not ever again subject the living to the same type of worldwide flood. This is the first statement of the fulfillment of the earlier pledge, the lasting Agreement, which was to be expanded upon further in the closing chapter of the narrative, Genesis nine.

The final verse of this Genesis chapter eight reinforces this pledge, closing with a third negative (here *shall not*) and containing a series of short, powerful contrasts:

> 8:22) "As long as the earth exists,
> Planting and harvest,
> Cold and heat,
> Spring and summer,
> Day and night,
> Shall not be taken away."

13

The Drying of Land

VARYING INTERPRETATIONS of words through the centuries have been examined, and now additional terms, each within chapter eight of Genesis will be reviewed, beginning with that common word: *window.* Here are two closely situated verses, with the first declaring the direct use and the second the indirect use of that opened window in the Ark:

> 8:6) After forty days had passed,
> Noah opened the small window
> Within the Ark
> He himself had built.

> 8:9) Noah, reaching out his hand,
> Took the dove to himself,
> And brought it inside the Ark.

On a craft in water, or on land, a window could open outward, as with a porthole. In Hebrew the original word *challon* meant *window*, one which would be built within a wall. The same Greek word, *thuris*, a small window, innately suggested that such a window, being small, would not allow much outside visibility, accommodating in this instance only a bird and an outstretched hand. With the Ark's upper sides suggested as tapered, any overt outside or downward observation could have, it implies, been compromised. Having a small window, either on a sloped side or facing directly upward, would explain to listeners why birds were sent out, as a bird, unlike people inside, could then, once set free, clearly scrutinize the surrounding area and determine if any land were evident.

From ancient times to the modern era, mariners throughout the world had used varieties of birds to assist in locating land. Individuals at sea would at times partially starve birds, release them, and then steer their ship in the direction of the bird's food-seeking flight in order to arrive at otherwise unseen terrain. A bird's line of flight could be used as a guide to a potential landing site.

After having sent out the dove three times, not until later does it say that Noah would see outside for himself:

> 8:13) Noah uncovered the roof
> Of the Ark he had built,
> And was able to see for himself

In this verse, another accessory of the vessel is mentioned, where Noah: "*uncovered* the roof." Here a word was utilized which differs from the earlier type of covering at 6:14, that is, the veneer sealant during the construction of the Ark. Instead, this latter covering, in the same verse disclosing the shallowing of the waters, was an item that could be removed, and as a separate feature it is mentioned only here, after the waters had significantly receded. The Hebrew wording for it first used a verb, *sur*, meaning to turn aside, to remove, and then continued with a noun, *mikseh*, defined simply as *a cover*, often of animal skin origin, used for tents, and has its first biblical mention in this verse. When used later, in Exodus, to describe the tabernacle, the large sacred tent, the same word refers to tanned animal skins or hides. *Covering* is used twice in the Exodus verse describing that tent:

> And thou shalt make a covering for the tent of rams' skins dyed red, and a covering above of badgers' skins. (Exodus 26:14, KJV)

In Greek, for unveiling the Ark, at 8:13 a verb was used, *apokaluptó*, meaning to uncover, and to bring to light, to reveal. Earlier in the Genesis chapter, at 8:2, that same verb was used for revealing the reservoirs and enclosures, and again, the word *apocalypse* stems from that root. An antonym of *apokaluptó* is *kaluptó*, meaning to veil, to conceal, and that verb was used still earlier at 7:19, where the rising water was "*overspreading* every one of the mountains." Here in this later verse the text states that Noah was uncovering or revealing the roof, or *stegé* of the Ark. That covering could, in today's terminology, be viewed as a type of tarp, used now to protect large equipment or even turf from the effects of weather. With its removal, this describes the first time Noah was to look directly outside, unobstructed, allowing full outward viewing since the Ark had been closed at the flood's beginning. After this observation, coming a month later when the ground had become fully dry, there came the instruction to depart.

Within this Genesis chapter 8, and the description of the gradual lowering of waters, an early reference to the lessening of the waters was in 8:5: "The peaks of the mountains had reappeared." Then, at 8:9, with the first return of the dove, it states: "Water still stood over the wide expanses of the earth." For this latter phrase, it had in centuries past been written as: "for the waters were on the face of the whole earth" (KJV).

Depending on the wording, this can be open to misinterpretation, with one verse stating that the peaks of mountains were already visible, and soon after another verse then spoke of water covering the *face* of the entire earth. This could, in current meaning, imply today that even the mountains were still under water, and that would appear to be a contradiction.

This arises because of a discrepancy in modern language when using the word 'face' in the expression: the *face* of the earth. The terms for face (Hebrew *panim*, Greek *prosopon*) each could mean a human face, visage, countenance, but it additionally meant flatter exterior surface, or external vista. The Greek *prosopon* contains the root *op*, as in optical, referring to what is visibly seen before one, through the eyes. The words *panim/prosopon* were also used early in the flood narrative, as *seen*, at 6:7 with "Any to be *seen* on earth."

Panim or *prosopon*, when elsewhere in the Bible, did often refer to a visible human face: "Joseph fell upon his father's face" (Genesis 50:1, KJV). They also have been translated, rather than *face*, as *before*, or *in front of*, when dealing with what was geographically larger, as with, and staying in Genesis: "and pitched his tent before the city" (Genesis 33:18, KJV). But when referring to the *face* of the earth, and in the present day, a different, and therefore at-odds impression can come about, especially of what could now be perceived as being completely over the round planetary earth.

A modern conception of the earth's *face* is not the same as the then more common ancient topographical imagery being depicted in this portion of the flood narrative at 8:9. Instead, back then it was of the lower broad surfaces of the regions. An accurate reckoning now would be as expansive oceans, with mountaintops seen arising above the water line, at the horizon. It is that likeness, of far horizontal vistas with some appearing peaks, that is the more authentic one for this segment. Visible mountain peaks would not have been in contradiction to that imagery of covering the earth's lengthy surface. The same type of phrasing could be thought of today as descriptive of wide open spaces, of panoramic spans, such as prairies, with mountain peaks far in the background.

Now using "over the wide expanses of the earth" can befittingly bring out that same 'face' representation.

Elsewhere, where modern conceptions are more in line with the ancient wording, the expression *face of the earth* is used, as in a closely following verse, that of 8:13, in which is discussed the continued drying of the lands, and the gradual descent of the waters.

Starting from their greatest height, that descent can be traced through chapters 7 and 8 as:

7:20) Twenty five feet
Above the highest peaks.

8:5) The peaks of the mountains
Had reappeared.

8:9) For yet, water still stood
Over the wide expanses
Of the earth.

8:11) Noah realized the waters
Were no longer extending
Over all regions.

The full listing of the upcoming verse 8:13, and the verse which follows it, connote the process of "the face of" the land around the Ark becoming dry, as the waters receded more completely. In the two verses there are three references to the water receding, to lowering, and to the land fully drying:

8:13) On the first day of the month,
The water had *receded*
From more of the world.
Noah uncovered the roof
Of the Ark he had built,
And could see for himself:
Water *was lowering*
Over the face of the earth.
14) In the next, the second month,
On the twenty seventh
Day of the month,
The land's surface
Had become *fully dry*.

Not uncommonly, a prior translational usage of one shared English term (as with Ark and with pitch and with window) had previously come about to replace what were once multiple ancient words. In earlier English translations, separate but connected original words here in these verses, 8:13 and 8:14, had both been translated as *dry* in describing the ground as the waters subside. *Dry* had often been utilized in these two successive verses, but the ancient terms were not entirely synonymous.

In Hebrew *charab* (*khaw-rab´*), referring to drying, was used twice in 8:13 (and not in 8:14) and relates primarily to land becoming desaturated, that is, that the surface no longer had as much deep standing water. In the first use in 8:13, it implied that all the world's grounds were being freed from the waters, ("receded") and then ("was lowering") when Noah could himself observe the area around him.

In Greek in that same verse, the phrasing also two times referred to the subsiding or ceasing of the water from the earth. The verb *ekleipó*, meaning ceased or coming to an end (as in *eclipse*, a lessening or a reduction), in regard to the water having retreated, was twice used to convey that the water was shallowing. First it was worldwide, and then with Noah himself observing the shallowing. *Ekleipó* linguistically had been formed as a combination of two words, one meaning *from out of*, or *away from*, and the other meaning *leaving*. The verb here in this verse, rather than a simple repeat, if perceived as oration, suggests two slightly different usage concepts.

The first use of the verb was from the narrator's large-scale perspective, enlightening the listeners to what was occurring worldwide. The notification was that the water, previously described in detail, was now receding everywhere (*gé*, the *world*, the *earth*, is also used twice in the verse). But the second usage of the verb *ekleipó* is then described as coming from the more limited personal point of view of Noah.

Having been described as enclosed inside the Ark, a person in that setting could not have known much about the dropping water levels, or how the earth looked, unlike the listening audience, who had been told all along.

Listeners would have understood that, after a flood, in areas of adequate drainage, water can actually be seen as pulling back, for example at shorelines over a few hours or less, as with outgoing tides. Describing the removal of the cover, and Noah's personally seeing land, one reciting that water "was lowering" before Noah's very eyes would have carried more meaning when enhanced by an orator's expressions in performance.

Continuing, in the next verse, 8:14, and at a time later on, for "fully dry," the word *yabesh* correspondingly was used in Hebrew, and it was then signifying a greater degree of aridity, that is, land with any vegetation would tend toward withered, indicating a later stage of dryness, to becoming parched. Greek equally utilized *xérainó* (*xay-rah´ee-no*), meaning dried up or parched. That same verb *xérainó* had also been applied for the same circumstance just a few verses earlier, at 8:7, where, with the raven´s departure, it "darted away, not to return until later, after the world *had fully dried*."

In Hebrew, that pairing of the congruent words, *charab* in 8:13, and then *yabesh* in 8:14, also was to show up later in the Bible, for example the two terms appear one after the other at Job 14:11 where it states: "and the flood decayeth and drieth up" (KJV).

The overall implication was that the ground's dehydration was proceeding gradually and in increments, as the water in 8:13 was receding and the land was becoming less wet and the water observably more shallow. After more passage of time, that process went further in the next verse, 8:14, to being *fully dry* over the earth. The progress sets the stage for the next verses, those stating that God interceded with instructions to leave the Ark, and then began to fulfill the earlier agreement with Noah.

14

Upholding the Agreement

THE COMMITMENT TO NOAH in verse 6:18 was previously examined: "I put forward this lasting Agreement with you" in this book's chapter 9 (The Affirmation). In Genesis chapter nine is the notification of the expression of that commitment, along with, in the early verses of that chapter, a redefining of the relationship of humanity within a newly restored world. The chapter begins with:

> 9:1) And God
> Delivered blessings upon Noah
> And his sons,
> And said to them:
> "Grow in numbers,
> Fill the world,
> Exercise authority over it.

With blessings extended, there also is the statement, made earlier at 8:17, essentially repeated: "Grow in numbers, fill the world." The word pairings for grow/fill in Hebrew were *parah/rabah*, and in Greek were *auxanó/pléthunó*, each rhyming. The same word combination occurs again at 9:7, to balance the segment.

In between, verses 2-6, beginning with "From here forward" articulate the new alignment:

> 9:2) From here forward:
> Aversion,
> A trembling fright
> Of you,
> Will exist within
> Every beast …
> 3) Each living creature
> Can now be food for you …
> 4) But if their lifeblood
> Still moves within …
> 5) So shall it be
> With your blood …
> 6) For anyone
> Ever to shed
> The blood of a human being,
> So shall that one's blood
> Be shed in return.
> It is thus,
> In the unassailable
> Image of God,
> I made mankind.

Here, 9:2 is restating Genesis 1:28, where animals were subordinated to humans ('have dominion over' KJV). In an alteration, food choice was expanded ("can now be food for you.") With that, an admonition, a precursor version of 'Thou shalt not kill' *(the Ten Commandments appear in full in Exodus 20)* is introduced here at 9:4-6, regarding the forbidding of the shedding of human blood, ending in mirrored form: "For anyone ever to shed the blood of a human being, so shall that one's blood be shed in return."

Verse 9:6 concludes with: "In the unassailable Image of God, I made mankind." For the word 'image' (Hebrew *tselem*, Greek *eikón*, meaning *icon*) the conventional one-word definition has been that, 'image.' But in language of the present, that word *image* carries a variety of meanings, many of them diminished in modern perception. The single term now will just as readily refer to a low resolution digital thumbnail rather than to an impressive representation, the latter of which those words of the past were characterizing. As with many terms of that prior era, today more than one word is needed to thoroughly regain the impact of one ancient powerful concept. Using "unassailable Image" more accurately secures the inviolability and extensiveness then being portrayed.

There follows the further fulfillment of the Agreement in the final verses of the narrative. The earlier pledge was now being upheld, and the rainbow was put forth as a symbol:

> 9:9)   I stand forth to uphold
> My promise made to you
>
> 9:17) That shall be
> The visible confirmation
> Of this decree

Genesis chapter 9 was written largely as chiasms, and the middle section of the chapter from those verses 9:9 to 9:17 will be shown now by using identifying letters, to better demonstrate that format. From a starting point at 9:8, a more complete and interwoven chiastic form unfolds, in a layout of AB-X-BA, with the middle X segment itself consisting of a smaller internal 'ab-ba' repeat. Here is that entire portion of the chapter, now with lettered labels:

9:8) Continuing,
God spoke to Noah
And to his sons with him, saying,

A 9:9) "Know this:
I stand forth to uphold
My promise made to you,
And to your descendants
After you,
10) And also to every living being
After you:
From the birds, from the livestock,
And all the wild beasts of the world,
As many as accompanied you,
All those sent out
From inside the Ark.
11) I shall stand by
This promise to you:

B "Never again shall all flesh cease
From the water of the flood.
Never again shall there be
A flood of water
To devastate the world."

X **a** 12) Then God
Spoke further to Noah:
"This becomes the symbol
Of that pledge
I enter upon with you,
And with every living creature,
As many as will be
For unending generations.
b 13) I unfurl my rainbow
Among the clouds,
It will be a display
Of the sacred pledge
Between myself and the earth.
b 14) And it shall be,
Wherever I gather clouds
Over the earth,

And a rainbow shall be seen,
a   15) Then I will remember
My promise,
Between myself and you,
And between every living being:

B   "Never again shall the water
Of a flood
Take away all that live.

A   16) "When a rainbow
Is in the clouds,
I will look upon it
And shall remember
The everlasting promise
Between myself
And the earth,
And between living beings
Of all flesh
Throughout the world."
17) And God said to Noah:
"That shall be
The visible confirmation
Of this decree
Which I have proclaimed
Between myself
And all the living
Upon the earth."

For summarization purposes, the nine verses 9:9 through 17 can also be restated in a shorter chiastic format, and paraphrased briefly as:

a) I confirm this promise,
b)   That I have made with you,
c)   And all creatures that will live,
d)   With this rainbow in the clouds.
x)   When it appears, I do affirm
                That no flood will yet again
                Come to cover the earth.
d)   This rainbow in the clouds
c)   For all who yet will live,
b)   I have made for all to look upon,
a) This is the sign of that promise.

Falling between the genealogical listings of the Genesis chapters five and ten were the start and ending points of the flood chronicle. Proceeding further in chapter nine in Genesis, there was a continuation by stating that Noah went on to become a tiller of the soil, planting a vineyard. That next genealogical listing follows, comprising all of Chapter 10, and from there begins another account.

What can be derived from the Great Flood episode is that the entire earth, despite the error of human faults, was, in telling, given another chance, was permitted rebirth, was provided a renewal. This narrative, as with others throughout the Bible, was about catastrophe followed by recovery. It was about a massive undertaking, about directions being carefully followed, about the triumph of life, of human achievement.

As with other episodes of setback, and individual responses to those, this epic expanded upon that, to a worldwide scale. By having survived the deluge, Noah and his family served as a representative core, personifying a new beginning in their now different world.

The emphasis throughout the entire episode, that of careful and thoughtful deliberation, and then of actions and interventions, can provide enduring lessons, by serving to characterize the results of drawing upon elevated capability. At its conclusion, the delivery of the rainbow reinforced and symbolized the message that the world can be seen as beginning afresh after every rainfall.

In this translation, if more of what was the narrative's original harmony has been re-affirmed, and if aspects of its pacing and fullness have re-emerged, then a greater understanding of scriptural writing can come about. When the literal detail can be more clearly experienced through more comprehensible language, and when the terms of this time can better replicate the written patterns of thought of that time, then the richness of the long-ago text, and its subtext, can be better appreciated. To adhere to the original, to stay as close as possible to the ancient wording, and to use the vitality of today's verbiage to restore much of the lyricism that had been lost, has been my priority. A guiding tenet for me as a translator is: If it wasn't there, don't add it. But if it was there, then make it clear, to get it right.

The more understood this story, the more profoundly memorable the message. Lifting the curtains, one by one, of linguistic uncertainty has, it is hoped, explained some of the intricately woven texture of this ancient scripture.

As listed earlier in this book, I have summarized the entire episode as:

a) God observed, then decided:
   Those of wrongful living,
   Throughout the world,
   Should no longer survive.
b)   God selected Noah:
      To construct an Ark,
      To be stocked with animals,
      Each to be kept alive.
c)   A massive flood proceeded.

x)   Later, God ceased
            The rising of the seas.

c)   Slowly the water receded.
b)   God instructed Noah:
      All were to depart,
      To increase in numbers,
      That each may thrive.
a) God stated this Promise:
   Such a flood
   To encompass the world
   Shall never again arrive.

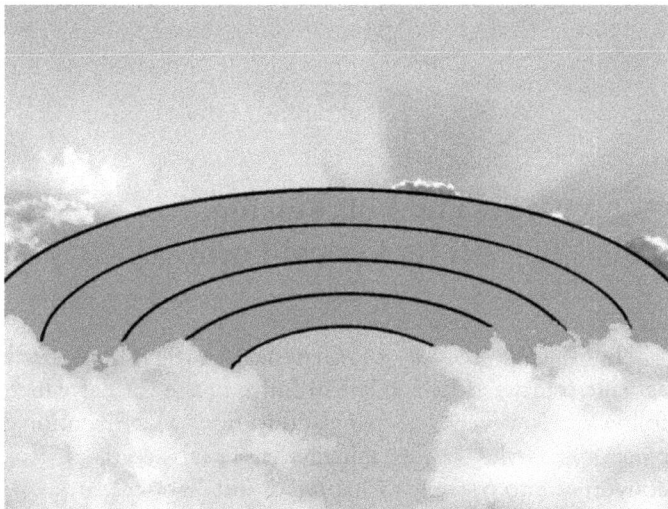

15

The Full Version,
In Its Lyrical Form

The Deluge section of Genesis, for this book, was actually translated first in lyrical form, in the format which follows. However, as many now find a conventional paragraph style to be initially easier to read, it was converted into prose for Chapters 2 and 3 above.

But when quoted, the more poetic format has been shown throughout this book, and this now is the full version, which more closely replicates the actual oral tradition, the commentary-like format of the original work. Beginning at Genesis 6:5, here is the Deluge narrative:

6:5 **The Lord God**
Began to look closely
At what was becoming
An intensifying hostility,
One inhabiting every individual,
All over the world.
Their course of thought,
Unfolding from within each heart,

Was of nothing but wrongdoing,
Day after day.
6) So it was,
That God reflected:
On having created
People upon the earth.
After profound deliberation,
7) God spoke:
"I am about
To sweep aside
Humanity,
Those I have formed,
Any to be seen on earth.
Gone
Will be the humans,
And further,
The animals,
From crawling beasts,
Up to the birds of the sky.
This,
The result of my decision
To have brought them
Into being."

8) However,
One
Had attained the approval
Of the Lord God.
9) There was Noah.
Noah:
Righteous,
A man of integrity
Among the others of his time,
Highly regarded by God.
10) Noah,
A father of three sons,
Named: Shem, Ham, and Japheth.

11) But still,
In the very sight of God,
Desecration
Was engulfing the world,
Deceit,
Overtaking the world.
12) The Lord God
Was witnessing
The earth's regions
Approaching ruin;
The one correct course
Was being utterly abandoned
By the many,
Those living all across the lands.
13) And it was then,
The Lord God
Disclosed to Noah:
"A breaking point
For human beings
Has been reached
Here before me.
It is certain that,
Spreading from them,
The earth
Is being severely defiled.
Now, listen well:
I bring an end to this,
To the world as it is.
14) For this reason
You, yourself,
Will be building
An Ark.
Begin with
Squared timbers of wood.
Bind together beams
To be aligned

Within the Ark,
And seal
With securing veneer
What will be
The inside and out.
15) You shall then
Lay out the Ark
To this:
Five hundred feet
The length of the Ark,
Eighty feet its width,
Fifty feet
To be its height.
16) To join together the Ark:
You will raise it,
And closely connect it
At its crowning point.
Also, a door
You shall install
In the side
Of the Ark,
And with
A ground floor,
A second floor,
And a third,
You shall
Make it ready."

17) "Know this:
I will be inflicting
A flood of water
Onto the earth,
To lay waste
To all beings
Which take in
Their breath of life
From beneath the sky.

As many as there are
Upon the earth,
Each shall meet an early end.
18) Yet, as to you,
I put forward
This lasting Agreement:
You will be permitted
To stay within that Ark,
You and your sons,
And your wife,
And the wives of your sons,
With you.
19) Furthermore –
From among
All the beasts of burden,
All the crawling serpents,
All untamed of the wild,
From all those that exist,
Two by two,
From every one of these,
You are to guide them
Into that Ark,
Where you are
To provide for them,
Male and female, alive,
There,
With you.
20) Of the birds,
According to their lineage,
Livestock,
Separated by their sort,
Creatures which crawl
Upon the ground,
According to their groups,
Two by two,
From all of these,
Will be approaching,

There,
For you to take in,
Each male and female.
21) And you are to gather
All types of food to eat.
Collect it together,
To sustain yourself
And each of them."

22) And Noah carried through
On every part of this.
What the Lord God
Had commanded of him,
He did accomplish.

VII

7:1 **And then the Lord God**
Said to Noah:
"You are to enter!
You,
And your entire family,
Into the Ark.
For under my observance:
You
Are of preeminent character
In the midst of these times.
2) Now – To the clean livestock,
Those,
Which are pure for ritual,
Those,
You shall guide in
Seven by seven,
Male and female.
But of the unclean,

Those,
Two by two,
Male and female each.
3) And even the birds of the sky:
Of the clean,
Seven by seven,
Male and female paired.
Of the birds unclean,
Two by two,
Male, female,
To assure
The spread of seed
Across all the lands.
4) It is to be,
In seven days,
I will deliver
A devastation
Of water to the world,
Forty days and forty nights.
I will wash away
Every entity I have made
From the entire surface
Of the earth."

5) And again,
All that the Lord God
Commanded of him,
Noah accomplished.
6) This,
While Noah himself
Was six hundred
Years of age,
And the earth
About to be subjected
To a crushing deluge.

7) Nonetheless,

Noah,
With his sons,
And his wife,
And his sons' wives,
Made their way
To within the Ark,
To hold out
Against the waters
Of the forthcoming flood.
8) Also,
From among
The clean birds of flight,
And the unclean birds,
Of the clean livestock,
And livestock unclean,
Of the clean wildlife,
And the unclean,
9) They went into the Ark,
In toward Noah,
Male and female,
Each two by two,
In accordance with
The directives of God.
10) And so,
After seven days,
The tumultuous flood
Was set in force
Upon the world.
11) It being
The six hundredth year
Of Noah's life,
In its second month,
On the twenty seventh day
Of the month,
On that day:
Burst apart
All the bulging reservoirs

Buried deep below,
And towering enclosures
Holding oceans above the skies
Flung open.
12) Waters were released
Onto the earth,
Forty days and forty nights.

13) During that first day,
Having entered
Into the Ark were:
Noah,
His sons Shem, Ham, Japheth,
And Noah's wife,
And the three wives
Of his sons.
14) And then,
Every untamed beast
By their species,
All livestock
By their sort,
Crawling creatures
By their categories,
Winged birds
From their flocks,
15) They came,
Conducted by Noah,
Into the Ark,
Two by two,
Male and female,
From all branches
Of beings
Which embody
The breath of life.
16) Those entering,
Each male and female,
Each entity of existence,

Embarked
In the same manner
As God
Had directed
To Noah.
And with that,
The Lord God
Shut the Ark
From the outside.

17) The flooding kept on
Those forty days
And forty nights.
The waters advanced,
Uplifting the Ark,
Elevating it
High above the surroundings.
18) The unrestricted overflow
Ranged ever further,
Immersing the lands,
Carrying the Ark
Upon its waves.
19) The waters,
Seemingly without end,
Came to conceal
The expanses,
Overspreading every one
Of the mountains
Under the heavens.
20) The levels grew
To twenty five feet
Above the highest peaks.
21) And so perished
The living
Which had before
Been active
Across the vast regions:

Birds,
Livestock,
Animals of the wild,
Crawling serpents,
All which moved
Over the surface,
And with them,
Every person.
22) They that had breathed
With spirit of life,
They, anywhere
Upon the lands,
All passed away.
23) Taken from existence
Was their every trace
Off the face of the earth:
From humans,
Animals,
Crawling serpents,
And birds of the sky.
None any longer
Were alive in the world.
Only remaining
Were Noah,
And those with him,
Inside the Ark.

24) And the waters
Stood at those heights
Upon the earth
One hundred and fifty days.

VIII

8:1 **And it was,** that God
Came to bring back to mind:
  Noah,
  All the untamed beasts,
  All the livestock,
  All the winged birds,
  All the crawling serpents,
  The many, there with him,
  Inside the Ark.
And it was then, that God
Proceeded to bring forth:
  A transcendent
  Breath of wind
  Across the world,
  Which calmed the water.
2) And so,
Were set firm:
Both the reservoirs
From the deep below,
And the enclosures
Above the sky.
Further inundation
From the heavens
Was held back.

3) It followed,
That after
One hundred and fifty days,
The waters
Coursing over the earth
Then were drawing away,
Their levels
Dropped lower.
4) In the seventh month,
On the twenty seventh day,

The Ark
Came to a halt
Above the mountains
Of Ararat.
5) With lapping waters
In gradual decline,
And when the passing days
Reached the first
Of the tenth month,
The peaks of the mountains
Had reappeared.
6) There,
After forty days had passed,
Noah opened the small window
Within the Ark
He himself had built.
7) He released one raven,
One, to see how much
The waters were reduced.
But it only darted away,
Not to return until later,
After the world
Had fully dried.
8) So he sent out a dove
To succeed it,
To discover if water
Was withdrawn from the land.
9) When the dove
Could not catch sight
Of any resting place to perch,
It flew back to him
At the Ark,
For water still stood
Over the wide expanses
Of the earth.
Noah, reaching out his hand,
Took hold of the dove,

And brought it
Inside the Ark.
10) After waiting seven days,
He again released the dove.
11) When it came back
With a fresh olive leaf in its beak,
Noah realized the waters
Were no longer extending
Over all regions.
12) He waited another seven days,
Once more sent out the dove,
And that time
It did not return.
13) And it came to be,
Noah reached in his life
The age of six hundred and one.
In that same month,
On the first day of the month,
The water had receded
From more of the world.
Noah uncovered the roof
Of the Ark he had built,
And could see for himself:
Water was lowering
Over the face of the earth.
14) In the next, the second month,
On the twenty seventh
Day of the month,
The land's surface
Had become fully dry.
15) Then the Lord God
Spoke to Noah, saying:
16) "Proceed forth,
Out from the Ark:
You,
Your wife,
Your sons,

Your sons' wives with you!
17) And all the living:
The birds,
The livestock,
The wild animals of the ground,
Lead them out as well.
Then,
Grow greater in numbers,
Spread throughout the earth!"
18) And emerged:
Noah and his wife, and his sons,
And the wives of his sons with him.
19) And every wild beast,
The livestock, the winged birds,
The crawling creatures,
According to their type,
All departed the Ark.
20) Then Noah
Built an altar to the Lord.
He selected from among
All the clean livestock,
And from among
All the clean birds,
And set those
As burnt offerings
Upon that sacred place.
21) The Lord
Sensed the sweet fragrance,
And thus
The Lord God decided:
"In giving thought,
I will not
Compound the condemnation
Of the lands of the earth,
Despite the dealings
Of humanity.
And while the notions

Of human beings
Still incline toward
The wrongdoing of youth,
I will not again
Strike down
All the living
In such manner,
As I have done.
22) As long as the earth exists,
Planting and harvest,
Cold and heat,
Spring and summer,
Day and night,
Shall not be taken away."

IX

9:1 **And God**
Delivered blessings upon Noah
And his sons,
And said to them:
"Grow in numbers,
Fill the world,
Exercise authority over it.
2) From here forward:
Aversion,
A trembling fright of you,
Will exist within
Every beast of the land,
Every bird of the sky,
In all which slide
Along the ground,
To within the fish
Of every sea.
Into your hands,

I offer them.
3) Each living creature
Can now be food for you,
As have been
The fields of vegetables
I had placed before
All of you.
4) But if their lifeblood
Still moves within,
Do not eat of them.
5) So shall it be
With your blood,
Yours,
Of your very soul,
Were it to be slashed
From within you
By the claw of any savage animal,
I shall hold that beast to account.
And just as much so,
Were it, from any person,
To be spilled by the hand
Even of one's brother,
I shall hold that man to account.
6) For anyone
Ever to shed
The blood of a human being,
So shall that one's blood
Be shed in return.
It is thus,
In the unassailable
Image of God,
I made mankind.
7) But now, you yourselves:
Grow in numbers,
Multiply, spread out
And fill the earth."
8) Continuing,

God spoke to Noah
And to his sons with him, saying,
9) "Know this:
I stand forth to uphold
My promise made to you,
And to your descendants
After you,
10) And also to every living being
After you,
From the birds,
From the livestock,
From all the wild beasts of the world,
As many as accompanied you,
All those sent out
From inside the Ark.
11) I shall stand by
This promise to you:
Never again shall all flesh cease
From the water of the flood.
Never again shall there be
A flood of water
To devastate the world."
12) Then God
Spoke further to Noah:
"This becomes the symbol
Of that pledge
I enter upon with you,
And with every living creature,
As many as will be
For unending generations.
13) I unfurl this rainbow
Among the clouds,
It will be a display
Of the sacred pledge
Between myself and the earth.
14) And it shall be,
Wherever I gather clouds

Over the earth,
And a rainbow shall be seen,
15) Then I will remember
My promise
Between myself and you,
And between every living being:
Never again shall the water
Of a flood
Take away all that live.
16) When a rainbow
Is in the clouds,
I will look upon it
And shall remember
The everlasting promise
Between myself
And the earth,
And between living beings
Of all flesh
Throughout the world."
17) And God said to Noah:
"That shall be
The visible confirmation
Of this decree
Which I have proclaimed
Between myself
And all the living
Upon the earth."
18) The sons of Noah
Who departed the Ark
Were Shem, and Ham, and Japheth.
Ham was the father of Canaan.
19) And these three,
The sons of Noah,
Were from whom
Their descendants disbursed
Throughout the lands.

ABOUT THE AUTHOR

With honors degrees in both History and Education, author/translator Daniel Eltzroth has been bridging the gap between ancient writings and modern language, clarifying those works for today's readers. He is also the author of *The Gospel of Thomas: Lost Sermons of Jesus Restored.*

DELUGE: THE GREAT FLOOD OF THE BIBLE

www.ingramcontent.com/pod-product-compliance
Lightning Source LLC
Chambersburg PA
CBHW060240050426
42448CB00009B/1534